The Internet: A New Marketing Tool

1999 Edition

Raymond D. Frost
Central Connecticut State University

Judy Strauss
University of Nevada-Reno

Prentice Hall
Upper Saddle River, NJ 07458

Acquisitions editor: *Whitney Blake*
Associate editor: *John Larkin*
Interior design and formatting: *Theresa Festa*
Cover design: *Lorraine Castellano*
Advertising copy and design: *Eve Adams*
Production manager: *Richard Bretan*

A Simon & Schuster Company
Upper Saddle River, New Jersey 07458

Printed in the United States of America

10 9 8 7 6 5 4 3 2 1

ISBN 0-13-011415-4

What's Inside

Preface

The Internet's rapid growth is reminiscent of television's early years. Something important and historic is happening; we are in the middle of a story with an unpredictable outcome. Users world-wide are adopting the Net at an incredible rate, companies are jumping on the bandwagon to display their wares, but cybercritics call the Net a waste of money and time. It has been some time since we've had something this exciting to debate!

We believe that the Internet is emerging both as an extremely useful tool for business planning and also as part of a company's marketing mix. As tools, the Internet search and resource sites can aid any discipline by opening a high-speed gateway to a wealth of information. Also, the Net assists with text-based communication: One-to-one e-mail conversation and e-mail conferencing via news groups and mailing lists. In the marketing discipline, the Internet serves as distribution channel, communication medium, and fertile ground for new products. Marketers use the Net for direct distribution of digital products, for electronic storefronts, and for distribution channel member collaboration. The Net marketing communication function includes advertising, public relations and sales promotion. Finally, Internet technologies created the opportunity for a variety of innovative services including search engines, stock trading, and interactive games. What's next?

The third edition of *The Internet: A New Marketing Tool* rests on this vision of the Net. Improvements in the third edition include:

- A comprehensive update of all Web sites
- More focus on critical thinking
- A leveraging technology sidebar in each chapter which explains how technological innovations are turned into business opportunties

Workbook Pedagogy

1. Principles of marketing. This workbook is designed to accompany a principles of marketing text. Both its content and organization reflect this design. Each chapter can be assigned as a stand-alone exercise, not requiring information from previous chapters. We recommend that students complete the search exercises in Chapter 1, however, so that their work in subsequent chapters will be more efficient. Teaching search strategies is "teaching them to fish" the Net.

2. Chapter structure. Each chapter begins with a short description of the topic and how it relates to marketing on the Internet. This is followed by an exercise. Each exercise begins with learning objectives, provides short explanations of various Web sites, and presents a series of questions interspersed with more explanations. The chapters conclude with summary questions enabling students to apply exercise findings to other situations.

3. Active learning. When students actively participate in the learning process, learning is enhanced. Through the hands-on approach in this workbook, students discover solutions to real marketing problems and in the process gain insight and experience with Internet navigation and content.

4. Guided exploration. Students are directed to particular Web sites and asked to answer questions. In this way active learning is directed learning. For example, we describe the Net as a distribution channel and then send them to Music Boulevard to go shopping for CD's. To answer the questions, students must find information at the site and offer opinions about findings.

5. Application and analysis. In many exercises, students must analyze the information from Web sites to answer marketing questions. One chapter focuses on Net users, directing students to sites reporting on demographics, geographics, psychographics and Net behavior. We ask students to describe the profile of a typical Net user and then to design an online magazine which would appeal to that user.

6. Net experience. We assume that users of this workbook are fairly inexperienced but know how to log on and use a graphical Web browser. There are many other helpful books if this is not the case with your students. We have tried to make our instructions generic enough so that any browser may be used.

We strongly recommend that you remain flexible while using this workbook. By the time you introduce it, many sites may have changed (see the FAQ, "Why there are mistakes in this book"). Nevertheless, our experience is that inventive students will find alternative solutions to most exercise problems. For example, in one class students were exploring the Net as an online storefront, and the site they were trying to access was down. While waiting, one student asked to order pizza over the Net. The class spent the next 15 minutes trying to find an electronic storefront to order food for the class. This exercise familiarized students with the use of search engines. It is this sort of discovery learning which sparks excitement and provides value to instructors and students. After all, we are all students of marketing, and nowhere is this so evident as with the Internet.

BUS 401 -- Marketing in Cyberspace

This workbook evolved from our interdisciplinary class, "Marketing in Cyberspace," which we have taught continuously since summer 1995. Faculty from two departments (management information systems and marketing) in the School of Business developed the course. From the MIS perspective, students examined the technical issues involved in locating and retrieving information from cyberspace, as well as issues involving ethics and Web page design. From the marketing viewpoint, students explored Internet consumer characteristics and behavior, and their effect on Web page content design. They also considered the Internet as a tool for marketing planning and both as a distribution channel and promotion medium.

An interesting aspect of this class is that the Web server served as our office "water cooler." Students and faculty gathered around for communication, virtually, that is. Although we met in a traditional computer lab classroom, all class materials were available online and we had a class newsgroup and an electronic newsletter distributed via e-mail. Occasionally, students e-mailed Web materials to share with the class, which were put on the server. The course grew and changed in real time such that students would log in and download an exercise only to find a new and improved version 20 minutes later. The course materials simulated the Net with respect to change!

In the first years of the course we had three evaluation instruments, each worth one-third of the grade. First, students took an exam based on course materials. Second, they developed a research paper on a topic related to Net Marketing. Third, students designed and created personal Web sites. Their sites were accompanied by a brief marketing plan that described their target market, and demonstrated how their page added value to the Net. All student papers and Web pages were put on our Web server for the world to view. Recently we dropped the exam and focused more on critical thinking and oral and written communication skills. Students summarize current articles, submit to the class newsgroup, and respond to the articles of others. We also ask students to present their papers and Web sites to the rest of class in a professional manner.

This workbook contains the exercises we developed for the class. Excluded are two components: Net ethics (privacy and copyright), and Web page development (offer implementation). The following exhibit outlines our course.

Topic	Learning Objective	Exercise
Introduction	Understand what the Internet is, how to connect, and test the waters.	Send e-mail to instructor.
Search strategies	Use the Web search engines and intuition to quickly find appropriate information.	Beginning search using Yahoo!'s subject tree Intermediate search using AltaVista. Deduce domain names.
Secondary data	Apply search strategies to find Web sites with information about a firm's macroenvironment.	Research the market for a new car by checking these Web sites: US Census, American Demographics, competitor pages, newsgroup discussions about cars, CIA Factbook, and US Patent Office.
Primary data	Learn how the Web and e-mail are used for primary data collection, and understand their strengths and limitations.	Register at HotWired and evaluate the purpose of information they request. Observe newsgroup product discussion. Write an e-mail questionnaire and discover how to collect a sample from newsgroups.

Net audience	Explore several sites with survey results describing Net users, and use the information to plan a new product.	Answer specific questions about Net user demographics, geographics, and Web behavior. Take the iVALs survey online and describe Net user psychographics. Discover Web market size and make future projections. Using the above information, plan a new Zine (Web magazine)
Ethics	Explore issues of privacy and intellectual property on the Net.	Take sides on several specific issues and debate in class.
Product planning	Understand domain naming problems and relate that to brand naming.	Select a domain name for a new Web site and search to see if that name is available.
Distribution channel	Experience the Web as retail store and direct distribution channel.	Visit an online storefront, select items and place them in a shopping basket. Discuss the Web as direct channel for software downloads and publications.
Communication Medium	Evaluate the Web for advertising, sales promotion and public relations.	Calculate prices for online advertising. Enter an online sweepstakes. Visit Rollerblade and see how the Web is used for PR.
Price planning	Use the Web for evaluating competitive pricing.	Visit Expedia and, using their database, analyze airfare pricing structures
Offer Implementation	Integrate previous knowledge and skills to create a Web site.	Write a brief marketing plan for a new Web site Develop a personal Web site.

About the Authors

Raymond Frost and Judy Strauss have collaborated on several Web-based projects. In 1995 they developed a Web server and site for the School of Business at Central Connecticut State University. As Web sites do, it expanded to many pages, including individual pages containing their course syllabi and related materials. They have published academic papers on issues of Web audience measurement, Internet survey research, consumer/company e-mail communication, and Internet pedagogy. In addition, they have developed Web training seminars for business clients. They also developed a new course, "Marketing in Cyberspace," the exercises for which serve as the basis for this workbook. Prentice Hall will publish their new comprehensive textbook for Marketing on the Internet classes in January 1999.

Raymond Frost is Professor of Management Information Systems. He has published scholarly papers on database management and is an associate editor of *The Journal of Database Management*. Frost has ten years of experience managing university computer laboratories. He currently teaches marketing in cyberspace, database and telecommunications courses. Frost earned a doctorate in business administration and an MS in computer science at the University of Miami, and received his BA in philosophy at Swarthmore College.

Judy Strauss is Associate Professor of Marketing. She has published academic papers in Internet marketing, advertising and marketing education. She has had many years of professional experience in marketing, serving as entrepreneur as well as marketing director of two firms. She currently teaches marketing in cyberspace and marketing communications. Strauss earned a doctorate in marketing at Southern Illinois University, and a finance MBA and marketing BBA at University of North Texas.

Dedications

To our students who make teaching its own reward

Judy

To my father--Robert Snoyer

Raymond

To my parents--June and Raymond Frost

Frequently Asked Questions (FAQ)

The introduction to this text is a list of Frequently Asked Questions (FAQ). Many sites on the Internet use exactly this format to help guide users and give quick, useful answers to common questions. Each Internet FAQ page begins with an index of questions. Very often, each question contains a hot button or hyperlink to its answer. Users scan the list for a question they would like answered and then jump to the answer. We have kept our list especially small so that you can jump in and get started. Once you develop search skills from the early exercises in this workbook, you won't need us to answer your questions: you can search the Internet for any information you need.

Index

What is the Internet?

The Internet ("Net") is a network of computers reaching every country in the world. It is similar in some ways to the telephone system. Just as you can call people anywhere in the world, so too can you contact their computers as long as they are connected to the Net. The Internet is more than computers and their contents: it is a social space where users communicate. It is this feature, as well as the fact that there is no governing body, that allows the Net to be shaped by its users. The Net is truly a grassroots development.

The Internet has been around since the 1960s when it was conceived by the Defense Department as a fail-safe way of messaging in case of a nuclear attack. As a result the Internet is quite robust--communications almost always go through--albeit rather slowly at times. From the '60s until the early '90s the Internet was used primarily by the Defense Department and by researchers in industry and education. It was used to grant shared access to distant supercomputers and as a means of sending electronic mail. In those days, the Net was fairly hard to use and it was difficult to find your way around. Outside of a fairly small community, not that many people knew of, or cared much about the Internet. All that changed in the mid-'90s.

This decade has been witness to a revolution created by three major developments, the birth of the World Wide Web (WWW or Web), hyperlinks, and graphical browsers. The Web and hyperlinks are two pieces of the same puzzle. The Web began as a standard that defined how to travel from computer to computer throughout the world by following embedded links in a screen display of written words (text). A click on the link and you were instantly transported to another computer as directed by the embedded instruction. Such clickable text was called hypertext. The Web and hypertext made it easy to get around; they formed a basis for navigation in cyberspace. What was missing however were pictures, icons, and color. People like a graphical interface since it is intuitive and easy to master. The graphics problem was solved by the development of graphical browsers; the most prominent browsers are Netscape Navigator and Microsoft Internet Explorer. Graphical browsers allow users to click on images as well as text links to navigate in a multimedia world. Not only can sites contain text and graphics, but they can also contain sound, video and even 3D video. Graphical browsers have brought visual appeal and entertainment value to the Web. The Web, hyperlinks, and graphical browsers have made cyberspace a very friendly place and have spawned the rush to get connected.

People are connecting to the Net at a phenomenal rate and the number of Web sites is doubling every 100 days. This creates two problems. First, the Internet is becoming slow. This is because communication lines over the Internet are shared. If 10 people use the same line, they each get one 10th of the capacity, or bandwidth, of the line. If 100 people use the same line, then their share is cut to one 100th. Similar remarks may be made about the computers with Web sites on the Internet (content providers). A computer that can handle 10 simultaneous accesses may come to its knees when 100 people try accessing it at the same time. Popularity in cyberspace comes with a price! Second, the Net contains so much material that it has become difficult for users to find their way around. It's no longer a global village; it's a major league city. Fortunately, there are tools that help. These are known as Web directories and search engines and they literally find Net destinations for you. Knowing how to use directories and search engines well is an essential survival skill in cyberspace. Consequently, we will dedicate the first two exercises to this topic.

Where is the Internet?

The Internet is everywhere. Since one means of accessing the Internet is by a standard phone line, the Internet is anywhere in the world that one can find a telephone. Once a user connects to an Internet computer, that computer serves as a gateway to the rest of the global network. Computers offering services on the Internet are scattered throughout the world. Fortunately, users do not need to know their geographic whereabouts while on the Net. All the user needs is the Internet address of the computer, not the geographic address in the terrestrial world. For example, the Internet address of the Central Connecticut State University (CCSU) is:

www.ccsu.edu

Reading backward from the end of the address, we discover that it is an educational institution (edu) named Central Connecticut State University (CCSU), and that it follows World Wide Web (WWW) protocols. Users connecting to this address are actually accessing files on a computer in Barnard Hall on the CCSU campus in New Britain, Connecticut, USA.

Most Internet addresses are not nearly so revealing as to location. It is not that the service is trying to conceal its location, but rather that location does not really matter. For example, does it matter to the user making an airline reservation that

www.americanair.com

is located in Oklahoma? Similarly, the user doesn't usually know the location of a business when dialing an 800 number. Internet addresses are like 800 numbers. One major difference is that 800 numbers are normally valid only in North America whereas Internet addresses are valid anywhere in the world.

How is the Internet Organized?

It is important to know that there are major Internet address classifications, known as top-level domain names. Each of them appears as the last item in an address (e.g., edu above) and can provide some information about the type of site to which one is connecting. The following are the largest top-level generic and country domain names along with the percentage of computer systems on the Internet using those names:

Domain	What it Means	Percentage in January 1998
.com	commercial	27.6
.net	Internet service provider	17.8
.edu	educational	13.3
.jp	Japan	3.9
.mil	US Military	3.7
.us	United States	3.6
.de	Germany	3.3
.uk	United Kingdom	3.3
.ca	Canada	2.8
.au	Australia	2.2
.org	non-profit organization	1.8
.gov	government	1.7
Total	(of 29,669,611 total)	82.8

Source: Network Wizards (www.nw.com)

Domain name knowledge can help you in two ways. First, it can assist you in evaluating the quality of information at a site. For example, government data at the US Census site www.census.gov (address ending in .gov) is different from information provided by corporations at commercial sites (.com). Second, if you are trying to find a particular site, you can often guess the site address by using the organization name and domain name. For example, the site for Coca-Cola is www.coca-cola.com.

Who is Out There?

We have compared the Internet to the telephone system: a global communication network of computers. You probably wonder who is sitting there at those 29.7 million computer systems, all glassy-eyed, using the computers.

Content Providers

First are the content providers. These are the businesses, universities, governments, other organizations, and individuals that allow others to peek into their computers. At CCSU, we have several computers that run 24 hours a day, and contain files that we created for others to view. For example, there is information about the faculty and the programs offered. We are a content provider, and we are definitely glassy-eyed.

Advertisers

Second are advertisers. These are the corporations that pay content providers for space on their Web pages. When you log on to a search engine's home page, for example, you generally will see announcements by advertisers who are paying for the space. This is how the search engines are able to offer their services for free. Topping the list is Yahoo! whose stock is now worth over $5 billion. Not bad for a site started a few years ago by two Stanford graduate school dropouts. Yahoo is a content provider and its paying clients are advertisers. In this guide you will have an opportunity to learn more about how marketers use the Web for advertising and other promotions.

Audience

Finally, there is the audience. These are people like us who surf the Web to find information from content providers that will be useful or entertaining. In addition to pulling data from Web servers, the audience also uses the Internet to communicate via e-mail. Even though we at CCSU are a content provider, as individuals we are also part of the audience. We use the Net both for business and for pleasure. We e-mail among ourselves and with others outside of the University, we post messages to newsgroups, and we surf the Web for our personal enjoyment. With the commercialization of the Internet, there is increasing interest in the characteristics and behavior of the Net audience. You will find information on this topic in several places in this workbook.

How Do I Connect to the Internet?

Users surf the Net via home, business, school, or the library. They are almost always charged a fee for this fun. In businesses, schools, and libraries the organization often pays the charge and even provides the computers. Home users must provide their own computers and pay their own way. Every Internet connection goes through an Internet Service Provider (ISP). These are organizations that buy very high bandwidth connections to the Internet backbone and then resell it (many times over) in smaller pieces to subscribers.

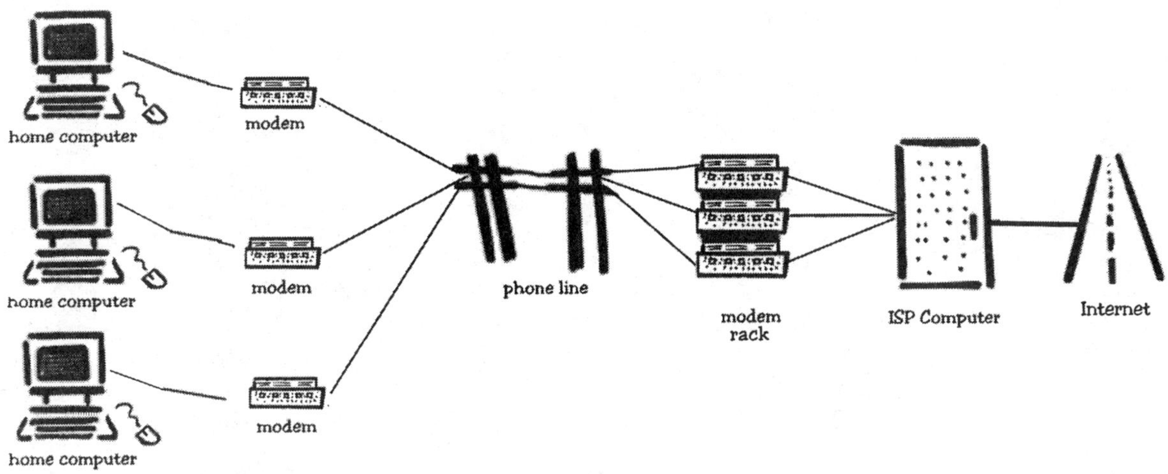

The connection from home to the ISP is typically over a phone line using a device called a modem. The modem translates the computer signals to sound waves, which are then decoded by a modem connected to a computer at the ISP receiving the call. Modems are an inexpensive means of getting connected, but they are slow. A recent technological advance allows modems to receive information off the Internet at a rate of about 50,000 bits per second (equivalent to about 5,000 letters per second). And while 50,000 bits per second is faster than any of us can read, the speed slowdown comes with sound and graphics. A full-screen picture can easily exceed 1,000,000 bytes (8 bits to a byte) and video requires changing that picture 32 times per second. Fortunately, some clever techniques (called algorithms) have been developed to compress sound, graphics and video to more acceptable quality, even over a phone line.

Some cable companies have begun to offer high speed Internet service over cable TV wire using a device called a cable modem. The cable TV wire into your home has a much greater bandwidth than a telephone line and allows for high quality video. Not to be outdone, some phone companies are rolling out a service called Digital Subscriber Loop (DSL) which will provide high speed connectivity over a standard phone line. The market will determine whether either of these become viable options.

The home user needs communication software and a web browser. The software is able to control the modem and maintain a connection with the ISP. Web browsers such as Netscape's Navigator and Microsoft's Internet Explorer are graphical user interfaces that operate over the established network connection.

The communication channel used by organizations typically offers a faster connection to the Internet and requires different hardware and software. These organizations normally have a higher speed line (greater bandwidth) into the Internet. However, since the high speed line is shared, as the number of users in the organization increases, the speed with which each communicates decreases accordingly.

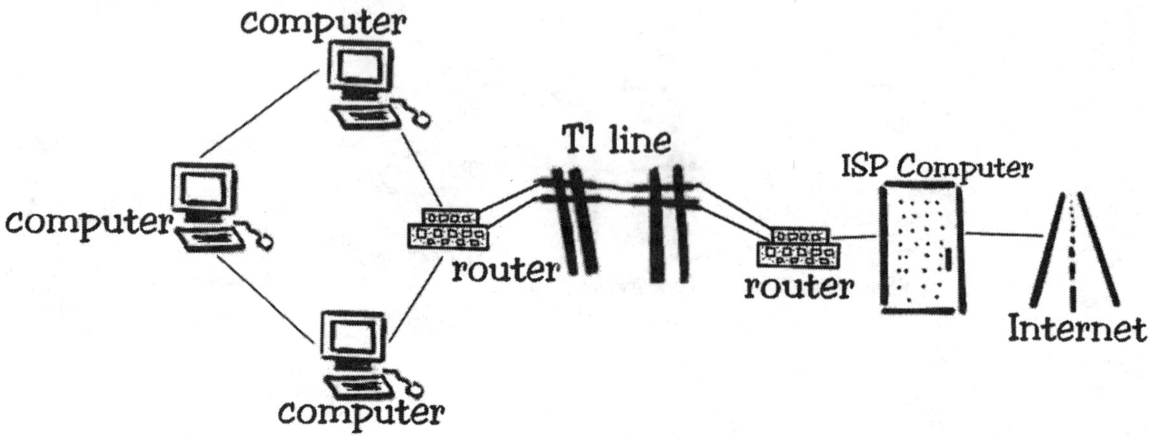

The business communications channel typically consists of a leased digital line (a T1 or fractional T1 line) connecting directly to the ISP. The T1 line connects to one computer on the Local Area Network (LAN) called the router. The router is able to direct signals to and from all computers on the network to the ISP along the T1 line. In this manner all users achieve an Internet connection by sharing a single line. For example, our computers at CCSU are part of the campus LAN and when we fire up our web browser and surf the Web, we are accessing the Net via our router. You will probably never see the router or T1 line since they are typically locked away in a wiring closet. The following table summarizes this information.

Component	**From Home**	**From an Organization**
Communications Channel	Regular telephone line	Fractional T1 line connected to a Frame Relay Network
Communications Hardware	56K Modem	Local Area Network (LAN) and a router
Communications Software	Dialer; Web browser	LAN operating system and a web browser
Computer (recommended specs--you can get by with less machine)	333 MHz Pentium II 64 MB RAM 8 GB Hard drive Sound card Speakers	Same

For home use, most ISP's charge monthly flat rate billing with unlimited access. The charge now averages about $15 per month. The largest ISP with 40% of the market is America Online, though it is not necessarily the most reliable. At one point they oversold their service to such a degree that users were constantly receiving busy signals. The situation actually led to a class action suit against AOL. Want some advice? Find someone who is happy with their service and follow their lead. Saving $2 per month is not worth the aggravation of bad service.

Business users pay significantly more per month since they connect at a higher speed. As prices for Internet connections for businesses are falling it makes little sense to enter into contracts for longer than one year. Since the price increases with the speed of the connection, it is best to buy less bandwidth initially as long as you can increase speed in the future without significant upgrade penalties. Advice for businesses? Hire a reputable management team to design your network, negotiate with vendors, and see the project through to completion. This way when something goes wrong (and it always does) it is the management team's problem and not yours.

Why are there Mistakes in this Book?

They changed their Web site, that's why! We created an exercise on a weekend and gave it to our classes on Monday, only to find it didn't work as planned. The home page we used had changed and our instructions suddenly became difficult to follow. This **will** happen to you somewhere in this book. So, what should you do?

One thing that might help is to understand the path system used in Web page naming. In one exercise we visit the site: www.cc.gatech.edu/gvu/user_surveys. The first part (www.cc.gatech.edu) identifies the host computer at that site. All pages at the site are contained in folders (subdirectories) of the host computer. For example, the information that you need is in the gvu/user_surveys folder. Fortunately, you rarely need to know in which subdirectory the information you are searching for is contained. A well-designed site will have a home page on the host computer at the top level (www.cc.gatech.edu) with links to all the pages on the site. So if www.cc.gatech.edu/gvu/user_surveys is not bringing you the information that you require, then simply back up to www.cc.gatech.edu and work your way to the information by following the links.

Another thing to remember is that there are many sources for some types of information. If something changes, try using the search engines to find another source that will answer the questions. This will really increase your surfing skills.

By the way, this feature of change is good. Content providers can continually update their pages and change graphics to keep them useful, without bearing the heavy costs of printed materials. They can experiment with new ideas at low cost and keep things fresh so consumers will be enticed to return.

How do Marketers Use the Internet?

The Internet is firmly established as a new marketing tool. Content providers offer valuable information to assist marketing planners. The Net has become an integral piece of the marketing mix, spawning new products and serving both as a distribution channel and a promotional medium for marketing communication. This is how marketers use the Net today, but with changing technology, the future is filled with potential!

Net as Planning Tool

Marketers use the Internet to gather data for marketing planning. The Net is similar to the library because much data exists on computers connected to the Net. These data help marketers understand competitors, consumers, the economic environment, political and legal factors, technological forces, and other factors in the macroenvironment affecting an organization. Secondary data on the Net are often more current than published data, and they are easy, inexpensive, and quick to access. However, because anyone can be a content provider, you should always do a quality check on Internet data. Marketing planners also use the Net to collect primary data about consumers. Through online e-mail and Web surveys, Web site registration, and observation of Net user discussions, marketers learn about both current and prospective customers.

Net as Product

One is constantly amazed by the creative products developed for this new medium. First there were the directories and search engines such as Yahoo!, Lycos, AltaVista, and Excite. Then there were products that would help a site be recognized by the search engines. Now products and services include online stock trading, ticket buying, classified ads, auctions, streaming audio and video, games, encryption services, payment services, and auditing services, among others. There are even services called "shopping agents" to help you find the right product at the right price!

Net as Distribution Channel

The Web is a place for online retailing. Many electronic storefronts and malls exist which allow users to browse and order products. In this way, the Net resembles a direct mail catalog such as the one you receive from J. Crew or the Sharper Image. Three major differences are:

1) **Cost savings**: the firm saves catalog printing and mailing costs. Additionally the retailer saves order entry costs since you are doing the order entry for them!

2) **Pull vs. push**: the users actively look for the retailer rather than passively viewing whatever catalogs turn up in the mailbox.

3) **Payment concerns**: users are currently more worried about giving their credit card over the Net than over the telephone--though this is changing. In the authors' own experience, the first few online orders feel quite adventuresome, but then it quickly becomes the preferred way to shop. Well-designed sites reassure the buyer by allowing a full review of the electronic "shopping basket" before executing the order and by taking steps to make credit card transmissions secure. Other enhancements include separate shipping and billing addresses as well as gift-wrapping and premium delivery options.

The Net is also a medium to distribute digital products. Software can be downloaded directly from the Net for free or for fee (e.g., shareware). Electronic magazines, music and video are also distributed directly over the Net, straight to your computer desktop. These activities reduce the number of intermediaries, thus shortening the distribution channel and significantly cutting an organization's costs.

Many electronic publications have recently adopted a push strategy (e.g. Netscape's In-Box Direct and Pointcast) in which the web page is delivered on a regular basis to your mailbox or as a screensaver just in case you forget to visit their site.

The Net also helps businesses in the distribution channel to collaborate in mutually beneficial ways. For example the bookseller, Amazon.com, has over 15,000 associates: these are other Web sites that receive up to a 15% commission for referring their users to Amazon for online book purchases. Electronic Data Systems (EDS), the information services company, uses a private computer network, called an extranet, for communication about products and activities with its distribution channel partners.

Net as Communication Medium

The Net is a strong medium for communication with target audiences. In fact, many believe this is the Net's main benefit to marketers. In this function it is similar to a magazine or television except that the Net allows two-way communication.

Corporations use the Web for the promotional purposes of advertising, sales promotion, direct marketing, and public relations. Some specific uses are:

- Maintain a Web site with information about products and services (content provider's "brochureware")
- Purchase advertising on other people's Web sites (advertiser)
- Build e-mail databases of consumers for communication purposes
- Hold public relations special events online (e.g., Windows '95 online anniversary party)
- Offer electronic coupons, hold sweepstakes, and conduct other online sales promotions

Chapter 1

Search Strategies

Searching the Net is a critical skill that you will use throughout this workbook. Your aim is to get to the information as quickly as possible. There are three steps involved:

1. Find the site

Find the site that contains the information you want. The computer could be located anywhere in the world. You use search engines and key words to find sites. The early exercises in this guide explain how to use search engines in detail. We discuss Web directories and search engines. We recommend beginning with Yahoo!, the premier Web directory. Yahoo! organizes the Web by categories and in this way gives you a view of related items. For search engines we recommend AltaVista. AltaVista searches more of the Web than does Yahoo!. This is good and bad--good because you get more results; bad because many of them are not relevant. You'll learn a number of clever techniques to improve the results of a search. Do not skip these exercises because they will save you lots of time on Internet research.

2. Find the page

Find the page at the site containing information that you want. Some sites have thousands of pages. Once you get there you could roam around for hours. Not a good idea unless you've got the time--we don't. Most sites have some type of index when you arrive to help locate information. Increasingly however, the larger sites are starting to include a search feature right on their home page. The search feature indexes all pages at the site and can help locate the specific information you want.

3. Find the text

Find the text on the page and hit the bulls-eye. Some pages are very long and can scroll many computer screens. For a very long page use the "find" feature of your browser to jump right to the text in the page that contains the target information.

YAHOO! Web Directory

Learning Objectives

- Define the appropriate uses of a Web directory.
- Distinguish between directory categories, sub-categories, and Web sites.

In this and the following exercise, you will learn techniques that greatly facilitate your ability to locate information on the Web. This is called Web navigation. Some of the navigation techniques are very basic. Others take some time to master. It is worth learning these techniques well, since they will increase your Net research efficiency and effectiveness.

This exercise introduces a Web directory. A Web directory is an index of a great number of pages on the Web, neatly organized by category, sub-category, sub-sub-category, etc. For example, Recreation⇒Automotive⇒Makes and Models⇒Porsche. Users navigate down through the directory until they reach a link pointing to a page that looks relevant. There is work involved in directory navigation but the results are often very relevant to the information needs. We generally recommend beginning with a directory for three reasons. First, people not software robots compile directories. The people provide some filtering by simply not listing sites that they deem useless. Second, directories will help orient your search by showing you which sites fall into the same category. Third, the premier Web directory, Yahoo!, is the most popular site on the Web and is very good.

Indeed Yahoo! is actually a bit of a hybrid between a directory and search engine. In addition to offering the ability to drill down manually through categories, there is also a search feature on Yahoo! that will show you all categories matching your search term. Furthermore, after showing you its own matches, Yahoo! will also offer you the option of transferring your search to other search engines for even more matches.

Oh, and by the way, a couple of graduate school dropouts from Stanford created Yahoo! A college dropout also founded Microsoft. Not that we're making any suggestions here...

Getting Started

A Web directory is an index to the World Wide Web organized by categories and sub-categories. It is very similar to the card catalog system in the library. The most comprehensive Web directory is Yahoo! Try it yourself! To start Yahoo! you need first to launch your Web browser. This will probably be either Microsoft's Internet Explorer, which looks like this:

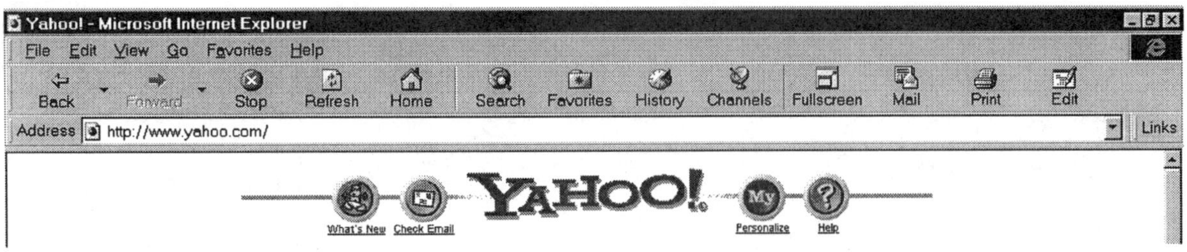

Or Netscape's Navigator, which looks like this:

Whichever browser you have, the most important button on the toolbar is the Back button, which always takes you back to the previous page that you visited.

To get to Yahoo!'s site you type: www.yahoo.com in the Address or Location line of your browser and then press the return key.

A Sample Directory Search

Let's imagine that we are interested in retrieving a list of companies that do marketing research about advertising on the Internet. Such a list would be a valuable resource for marketers. Using the Yahoo! directory we would approach this query from the general to the specific. The top-level category most likely to contain marketing is Business and Economy so we will click on that. Now follow the diagrams on the next two pages to see how the screen changes as we progressively select items leading us towards our goal of marketing research about advertising on the Internet.

Goal: retrieve a list of companies that do research about advertising on the Internet.

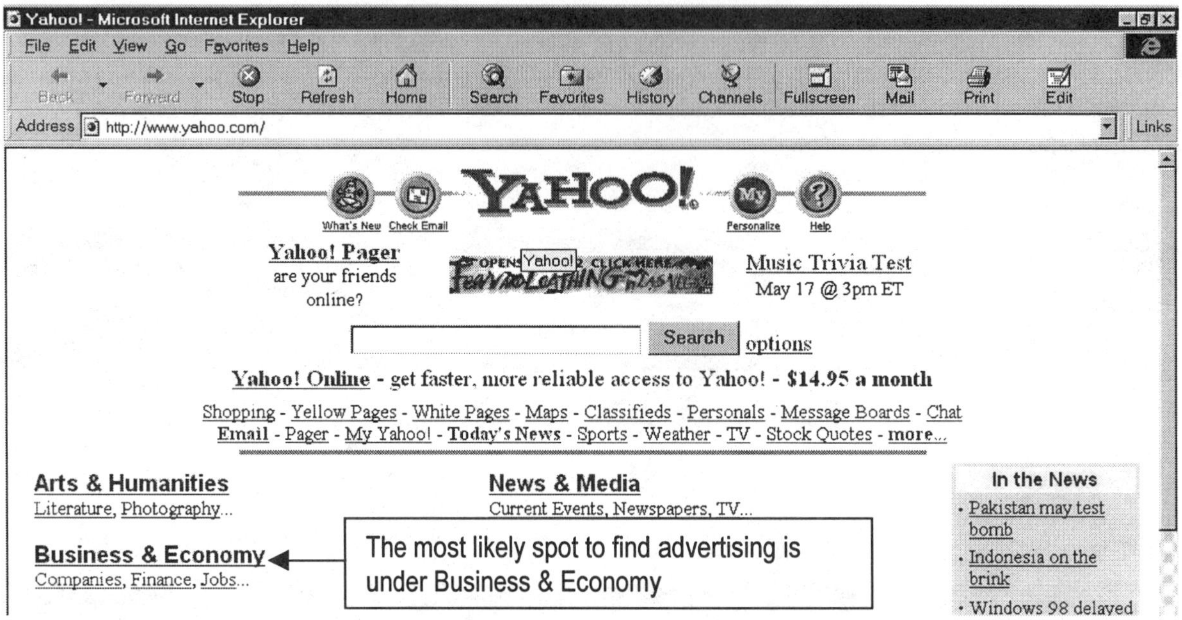

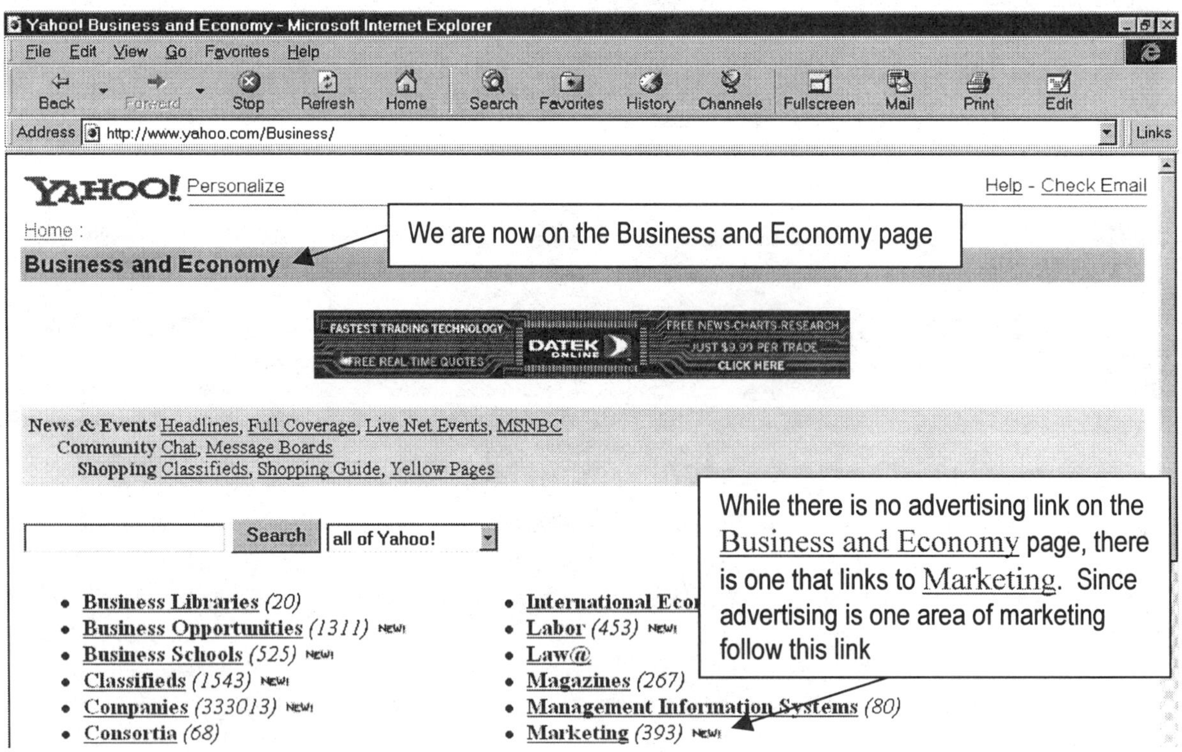

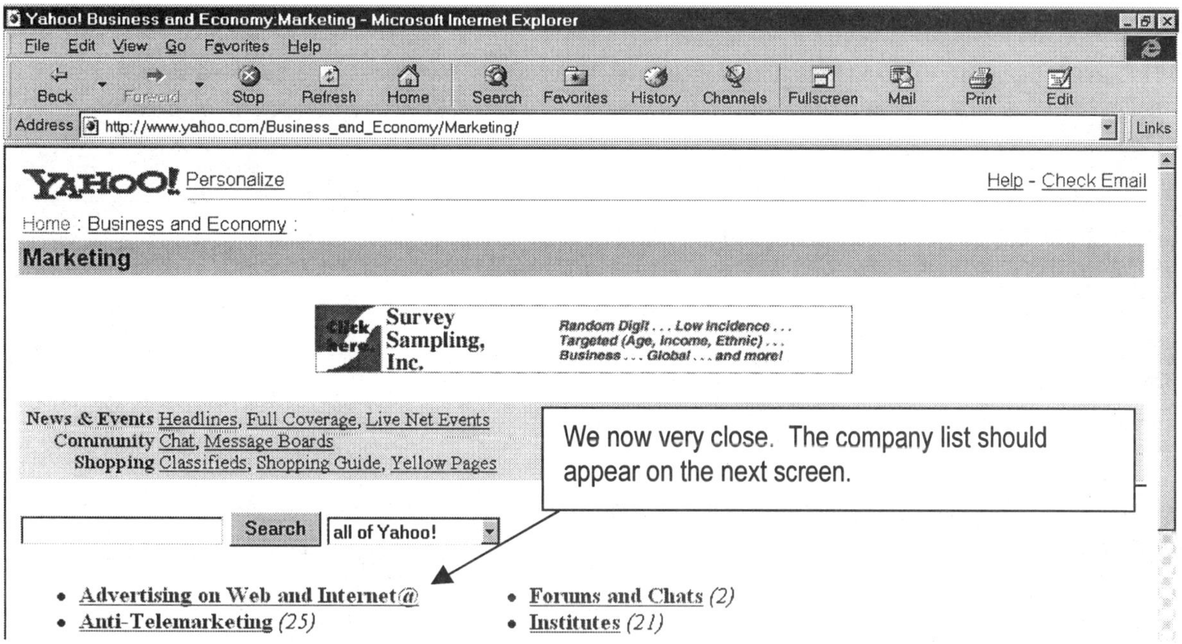
Yahoo! Business and Economy:Marketing - Microsoft Internet Explorer
File Edit View Go Favorites Help
Back Forward Stop Refresh Home Search Favorites History Channels Fullscreen Mail Print Edit
Address http://www.yahoo.com/Business_and_Economy/Marketing/
Links
YAHOO! Personalize
Help - Check Email
Home : Business and Economy :
Marketing
Survey Sampling, Inc.
Random Digit . . . Low Incidence . . .
Targeted (Age, Income, Ethnic) . . .
Business . . . Global . . . and more!
News & Events Headlines, Full Coverage, Live Net Events
Community Chat, Message Boards
Shopping Classifieds, Shopping Guide, Yellow Pages
We now very close. The company list should appear on the next screen.
Search
all of Yahoo!
Advertising on Web and Internet@
Anti-Telemarketing (25)
Forums and Chats (2)
Institutes (21)

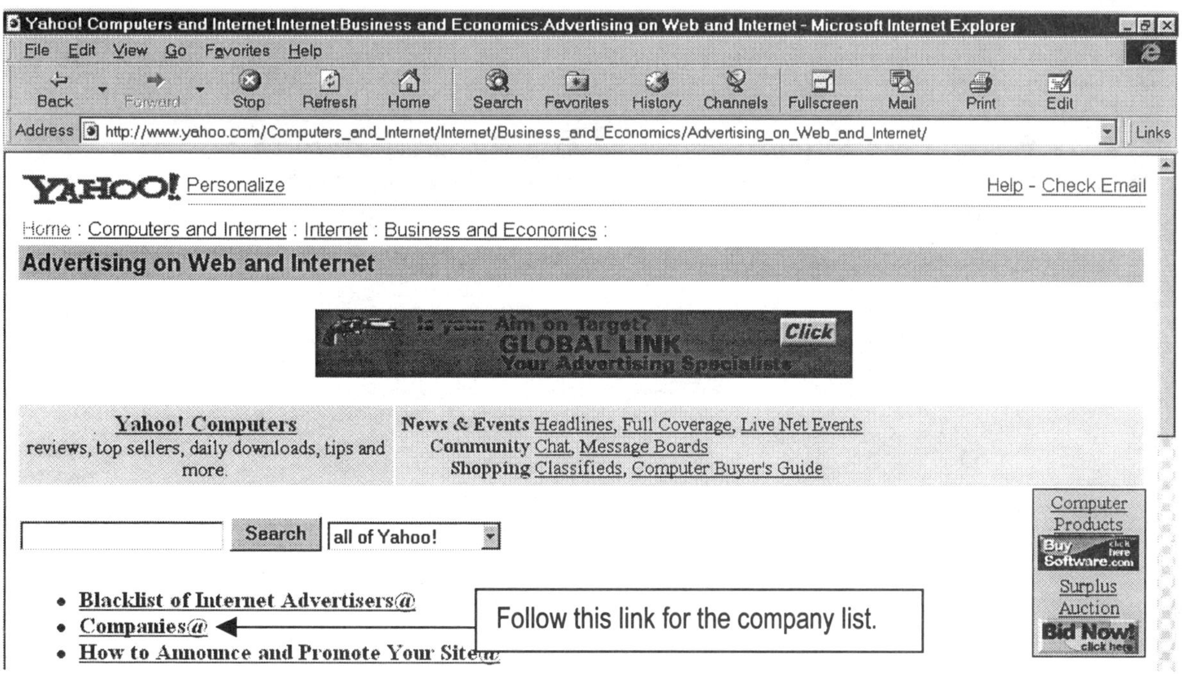
Yahoo! Computers and Internet:Internet:Business and Economics:Advertising on Web and Internet - Microsoft Internet Explorer
File Edit View Go Favorites Help
Back Forward Stop Refresh Home Search Favorites History Channels Fullscreen Mail Print Edit
Address http://www.yahoo.com/Computers_and_Internet/Internet/Business_and_Economics/Advertising_on_Web_and_Internet/
Links
YAHOO! Personalize
Help - Check Email
Home : Computers and Internet : Internet : Business and Economics :
Advertising on Web and Internet
GLOBAL LINK
Your Advertising Specialists
Click
Yahoo! Computers
reviews, top sellers, daily downloads, tips and more.
News & Events Headlines, Full Coverage, Live Net Events
Community Chat, Message Boards
Shopping Classifieds, Computer Buyer's Guide
Search
all of Yahoo!
Computer Products
Buy Software.com
Surplus Auction
Bid Now!
Blacklist of Internet Advertisers@
Companies@
How to Announce and Promote Your Site@
Follow this link for the company list.

For efficient searching, it is helpful to understand how the people at Yahoo! create their directory. At their home page, they list 14 general categories, under which all their catalogued Web sites are listed. A search begins with a general topic and "drills down" to increasingly specific topics. When assigning sites to categories, Yahoo! considers:

- Commercial versus non-commercial. **All** sites that sell something or are about companies that sell something are listed under Business and Economy⇒Companies. These same sites are probably cross-listed somewhere else as well, just to make things easier for you. For example, a company selling music CD's will also be listed under Entertainment⇒Music.
- Regional versus non-regional. An increasing number of Web sites are targeted to local audiences. Yahoo! lists **all** local sites under Regional so if you are looking for hotels in San Francisco you know where to begin searching. If a company is truly global, such as Apple Computer, it will not be in the regional listings.

Finally, you may wonder what the codes after categories mean. The number in parentheses indicates how many listings are in that category. For example, when we clicked on Business and Economy⇒Marketing in the above screen picture, you can see that there were 25 listings under Anti-telemarketing. But we clicked on Advertising on Web and Internet@. The @ sign means that this category is cross-listed, and if you look at our next screen picture, you'll see that clicking on it took us to listings under the general category Computers and Internet. It is not really important to know which category you are in at any one time, but it is helpful to understand that sites are cross-listed and that in a good directory you can find what you want using several different approaches.

Now we'd like you to try looking for your hometown newspaper by starting at three different general categories on Yahoo!'s home page. For each search, write the path you took:

1.

2.

3.

Incidentally, note that Yahoo! provides for targeted ad banner rotation. Banners are rectangular ads that are paid for by sponsoring companies. Look back at the previous Yahoo! screen pictures in this exercise and complete the following table listing the ad banner which appeared on each page:

Page	Banner Ad
Yahoo! Home	Fear and Loathing in Las Vegas
Business and Economy	
Marketing	
Advertising on Web and Internet	

Note the relationship of the advertised product to the Yahoo! category. Why do you think advertisers would pay a premium to use Yahoo!'s targeted ad banner rotation service?

A Sample Search

Yahoo! also provides the ability to search its site by typing in keywords rather than drilling down manually. This can be very useful especially if you don't know in which category to look for a given subject.

Goal: Find information on the Mazda Miata

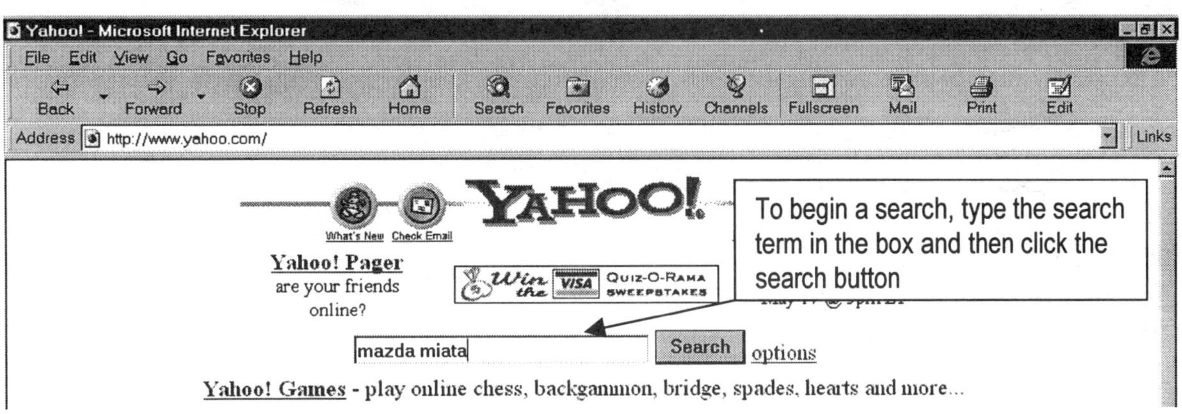

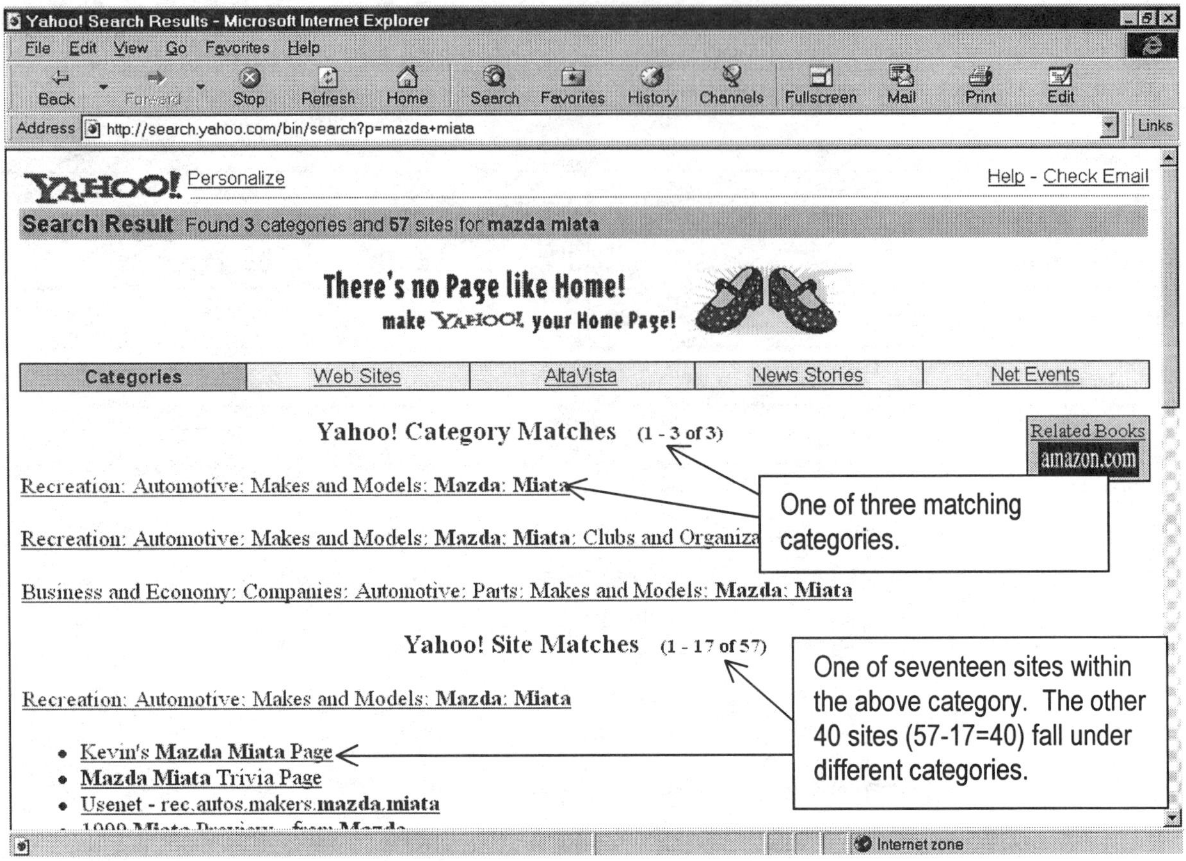

Using the Yahoo! search feature, conduct the three searches in the following table, which progressively narrow down a subject. Record the number of matches encountered with each search string.

Keywords Searched for	Number of Yahoo! category matches	Number of Yahoo! site matches
coupons		
food coupons		
grocery food coupons		

What conclusion can be drawn from this experiment?

Leveraging Technology

Megahubs and Games

The goal of every navigation tool is to become a portal of entry to the Web--i.e., the first place you start. Portals are sometimes called hubs and the really big ones are called megahubs. With 30 million unique visitors each month, Yahoo! is the king of the megahubs. Each portal or hub wants to become the first page that you visit when you startup your Web browser. (By the way did you know that you can select which page appears when your browser first starts up?) The more visitors they have, the greater the value of their advertising inventory. So in order to keep you coming back they have to offer more than just the ability to locate information. These additional services include customized weather maps, news feeds, games, stock quotes, TV and movie listings, free e-mail accounts and even Internet connection service! These additional services enable Yahoo! to differentiate itself from the competition. But technologically, how tough are they to provide?

The creators of Yahoo! realized early on that providing a search engine alone would not be sufficient to differentiate them from the competition. Their strategy has become one of creating a megahub--the first place users will visit when they sign on to the Web. If you look back at the banner ad on the first screen shot from the Mazda Miata search you will see the message "make Yahoo! your home page." In order to make this an attractive proposition, Yahoo! has introduced a large variety of extra services including e-mail, TV Guide listings, weather forecasts, directory assistance, and games. The games feature allows you to compete against and chat with other users all over the world in real time. This is a free service that gives you an additional incentive to return to their site. So how do they do it? Let's use chess as an example. If you select the chess game you will be given the option to play in one of the lounges--beginner, intermediate, advanced. Once you select a lounge a Java applet will be sent to your computer. The Java applet is the chess game. It will allow you to move pieces on the screen and will send those moves to your opponent's screen as well. So where is the game actually being played? Well, it is being played on Yahoo!'s computer called a server. Their server acts as a reflector taking your moves and reflecting them onto your opponent's computer. The server also acts as reflector while you chat with your opponent during the game. What you type will be sent to the Yahoo! server and reflected to your opponent's screen. Ever play chess? You spend a lot of time thinking and very little time moving. Therefore, Yahoo!'s computer gets a very light workout and can support thousands of users. So why provide this free service? We've already identified one reason--so that you will use Yahoo! as your point of entry to the Web. But there is another also. What do you suppose appears at the top of the chessboard? You guessed it--an ad that you will spend a fair amount of time staring at during the course of the game!

Search Engine

Learning Objectives

- Refine a search by including and excluding search words
- Use wildcard operators to broaden a search
- Refine a search by using quotation marks to force search words to appear together
- Construct a search which finds sites linking to your site

Search engines pull from the Web a list of all pages that match the search term that you type. This exercise will explore the AltaVista search engine. This exercise introduces some very powerful operators that will help you save tremendous amounts of time when searching the Web.

The last exercise introduced the Yahoo! directory. The Yahoo! directory contains all of the pages that the Yahoo! editors have had time to categorize. And while they have categorized a lot, the Yahoo! directory is far from complete. By contrast, AltaVista uses a spider program to search the Web and index documents by keywords. As a result AltaVista has a great deal more of the Web covered in its database. There are a number of spider based search engines like AltaVista. The reason there are so many search engines is that spiders are cheap whereas human labor is expensive. Because spiders work tirelessly day and night, they are able to visit millions of pages on the Web and index all the keywords that they find on those pages.

Pluses and minuses

Searching the Web means being able to specify wanted and unwanted search results. In AltaVista a plus means that you want the word to appear on a Web page, and a minus means that you don't. So +pizza -beer gives you all sites that have pizza but no beer. On the other hand -pizza +beer gives you all sites that have no pizza but lots of beer. Ready? Start up AltaVista by entering its address in your Web browser--www.altavista.digital.com. You should see a welcome page similar to this:

You now enter a search string in the box and then click the search button. Let's try our pizza and beer example. Be sure to include a space between the words, or AltaVista will think you are searching for one long word.

You Type	It Means
+pizza -beer	Find all pages that have lots of pizza but no beer

About how many documents were returned by the query?

Are you going to read them all? We didn't think so. Now try the second example.

You Type	It Means
-pizza +beer	Find all pages that have no pizza but lots of beer

About how many documents were returned by the query?

As you can see, with over 30 million sites covered on the Web, AltaVista is going to find a lot of stuff. Some of it will be right on target but most of it will be junk. Luckily, AltaVista tries to position the most relevant documents at the top of the list. So how does it determine what's relevant? Understanding relevancy will help marketers design Web sites that users can find. This explanation is taken from AltaVista's help screens:

What information does AltaVista actually index off of a Web page?

Basically, we index all the HTML information on a page: All text, ALT text for images, links (hrefs and images), anchors, title, description and keyword META tags, applet and ActiveX object names, the page's URL, its host name (www.foo.com) and its domain name (com). The treatment of Usenet postings is similar but with different keywords.

We do not index HTML comments.

How are pages ranked?

Results are ranked according to many different criteria. Among the main elements of a page that are considered in the ranking process are:

1. how many times query words appear;

2. whether the query words are in the title or META tags; and,

3. the proximity of query words in the document.

Can I make my site appear higher on the list when someone is doing a search?

There is no way to cheat. Simply make your page a better match for likely queries. Use common words that describe the content of your site early in your page. You can use the META tags to add a few invisible keywords. With the increasing growth of the Web, it will be ever more difficult to obtain a high ranking based on imprecise queries, such as "computer." Using AltaVista Search tools, however, allows users to construct much more precise queries, so you will get more value by making your page a good match for AltaVista Search queries.

Does your engine detect and penalize for spamming, that is, word stacking, spoofing, multiple page submissions, and the like?

Yes, we do spend a lot of effort on this. Our anti-spamming techniques are not based on content (i.e. we don't look for "sex" words) or review (too many pages). The idea is to find sites or subnets that submit large numbers of pages with essentially the same content, or leading to the same content. Depending on the offense, a designer may be warned or blacklisted from the AltaVista index. We are constantly fighting to maintain the highest quality index on the Web.

In spite of AltaVista's claim that there is no way to cheat, a cottage industry has grown up of companies such as www.webposition.com and www.did-it.com who try to find out exactly how the search engines perform their rankings and then help you engineer your page to achieve the highest possible relevance ranking within the rules.

Combining functions

While AltaVista places pages higher on its search results list when the search words appear close together on the Web page, sometimes you want them right next to each other with no words in between. To accomplish this we put the words in quotes. Let's say we are interested in pages on **web marketing**. We'll get better results by entering the search string **"web marketing"**. But what if we want to limit further to just those sites that mention the Nielsen Survey? Try it yourself and see what you get.

You Type	It Means
+"web marketing" +"nielsen survey"	Find all pages that have the words web and marketing where those words appear right next to each other. Those same sites must also have the words nielsen and survey right next to each other.

About how many documents were returned by the query?

You can get very specific!

WHEN IN DOUBT, lowercase

You may have noticed that in all of the examples above, the search strings were typed in lowercase even when searching for a proper name such as Nielsen. The reason for this is that lowercase matches both lower and uppercase whereas uppercase matches uppercase only. So, if some webmaster forgets to capitalize Nielsen, you'll still find that site.

A star for the wildcard

What if you are looking for information on **European** Travel Agents? It is reasonable to assume that **Europe** Travel Agent would also produce a good match. Rather than run two searches we can use the wildcard notation to match all words that start with **Europe** (i.e., **Europe**an) by typing **europe***. Try the following example:

You Type	It Means
+europe* +"travel agent"	Find all pages that have words that begin with europe. Those same pages must have the words travel agent right next to each other

About how many documents were returned by the query?

Who is linked to us?

On the Web, more is better when it comes to site visitors: more visitors means more potential business. Visitors can link to a site in many ways:

1. by deducing or guessing a site name, for example, www.coca-cola.com
2. by searching for the site using a search engine,
3. by copying the address from an advertisement or other media, or
4. by following a "hot link" from another site.

Interestingly, Coopers and Lybrand Consulting found that 39% of Web users learn about sites through other media, 44% through word-of-mouth, 32% through browsing, and 10% through "hot links" (source: cyberatlas.com).

We now focus on following a hot link from one site to another and begin with a fun exercise to determine which sites on the Web have a link to our site. The sincerest form of flattery on the Web is to put a link on a home page to another site. The more folks that do it, the more traffic to the hot linked site. What if we could find all the sites in the world that have a link to us? Well we can.

Let's see which sites link to the American Airlines home page. The address for American Airlines is www.americanair.com. The "link" operator will show us all sites that link to American Airlines.

You Type	It Means
link:www.americanair.com	Find all pages with a **link** to American Airlines

How many sites link to American Airlines?

Go to the first site on the list. Can you find the link to American Airlines? Where was it?

How can the list of sites that hot link to American Airlines help American's marketing efforts?

Interestingly, some search engines actually use the number of links to a site to help compute its relevancy ranking. Not a bad idea since the Web community is effectively voting with its links.

Nevertheless, links from other sites are not always welcome. Ticketmaster at one time sued Microsoft for providing a link to their site. Their gripe? The Microsoft link did not point to their home page but rather to a subpage. Ticketmaster wants to communicate with users through the "front door" perhaps so that they will see a full menu of products, promotions, and advertising.

Leveraging Technology

How Search Engines Work

The Web is a very big place with hundreds of millions of pages. Realistically it would be impossible for the search engines to search the entire Web every time someone types in a search term. It would take days to complete the task. So what do search engines do? They actually do the searching in advance over a long period of time. They send automatic programs called spiders out on the Web to go from site to site, page by page and word by word. These spiders build up a massive index or database of all the words found, where they were found, how many times they appear on each page, etc. It is this database which is actually queried when you type in a search term. Because it is an indexed database the query returns the results almost instantly. The results are generally returned in order of relevance with the most relevant site appearing first. But how do they know? It is the database's job to figure out which sites are most likely to be relevant to your search term. Here the spider aids it. The spider does more than just count words. It also looks for where those words appear on the page. For example, if the word is in the title of a page then it is given a higher relevance value than a word appearing in the body text. The spiders are also trained to avoid sites that attempt to trick them by repeating words more often. One technique is to ignore repeats that are not separated by at least, say, seven other words. This guards against someone loading their site with, for example, Mazda, Mazda, Mazda. The actual techniques used are becoming trade secrets since producing a search engine which returns truly useful results is actually a point of differentiation and therefore provides a competitive advantage.

Chapter 2

Market Analysis Using Secondary Data

Any computer connected to the Internet can be likened to a book sitting on a library shelf. It is there to be accessed and used as a source of information. A major difference is that the information available on the Internet is not censored, reviewed, or authorized by anyone other than the owner of the computer. This information is also manageable; it can be changed and updated at any moment. This, of course, leads to a great number of Web sites containing information of questionable quality. Nonetheless, there are many ways that the Internet is better than the library. It is open 24 hours a day, the information is often more current, and users have equal access from all over the world. This information is also quick to find, easy to download to your computer, and there are no fines or late fees (as long as you don't break copyright law!)

What type of information do marketing managers need that might be available on the Net? It is important to collect information about consumers, competition, and other factors outside of the organization. These data help to answer the question: What opportunities and threats are in the business environment for a particular organization and industry? Armed with this knowledge, marketing managers can plan products, pricing, distribution and promotion that better meet the needs of organizations and individuals.

In this chapter we focus on secondary data: information gathered by someone else who makes it available to us. Sources of secondary data on the Internet vary from the US Census Bureau to online magazines and research companies who provide statistics and analysis that help marketers make decisions.

Environmental Scan

To identify threats and opportunities, the corporation wants information about the macroenvironment in which it operates. An environmental scan seeks market information about the following:

- demographic trends
- competitors
- technological forces
- resource availability
- cultural trends
- economies
- legal and political environments
- other external factors which affect the marketing effort

page 38 - Secondary Data

Much of this information is available on the Internet: some for free, and some for a fee. The American Honda Motor Company exercise will guide you to many sources of free information. Remember to evaluate it by determining its source, timeliness and general quality.

American Honda Motor Company

Learning Objectives

- Apply appropriate search strategies to find information quickly on the Web
- Explore Web sites with information about the macroenvironment
- Understand newsgroups as a source of competitive intelligence

Automobile manufacturers are continually seeking information about changes in the automobile industry and its macroenvironment. This exercise focuses on the American Honda Motor Company www.honda.com and directs you to perform an environmental scan on their behalf as they prepare for a new product introduction. The product is the Honda CR-V. The car was introduced to the U.S. market in 1997 after tremendous success in Japan. It is a playful sport utility vehicle made for the younger generation.

Demographics

Is there a large target college population for the CR-V? An excellent source of demographic information on the web is the US Census web site. Like many government Web sites it is free and maintained by your tax dollars. Maybe they should sell advertising! While the official census takes place every 10 years, the Census Bureau maintains more current statistics from other surveys. We will use the Census statistics to study the size and composition of the college market. Locate the US Census Web site at www.census.gov. You should see a screen that looks like this:

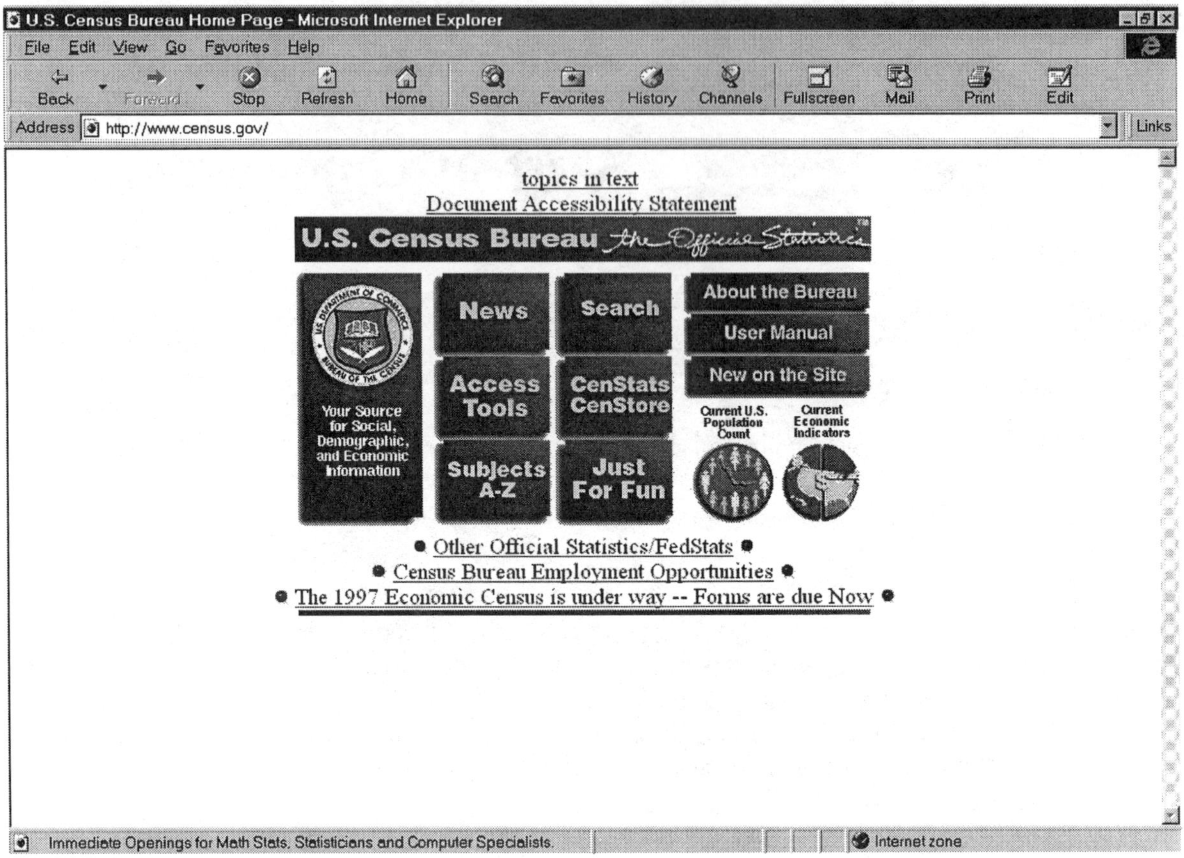

At the Census site, click on subjects A-Z. Next click on C and then find College Enrollments. Under Historical Tables click on Table A-7. College Enrollment of Students 14 to 34 Years Old. This information will help you advise Honda on the attractiveness for the college student target market. Remember what we said earlier about Web sites constantly changing? If the Census Bureau's Web site does not look like our screen picture, you can follow your nose through the new site to find the information for this exercise.

How many undergraduate students in this age group were enrolled in college during the most current year for which they have information? Caution! The figures listed are in thousands.

Is the trend up or down since the previous year?

♒

Which market is larger, the one for private or public school students?

♒

Is the market better for female or male students?

♒

Cultural Trends

How is the market changing? Would the CR-V appeal to its target market? Visit American Demographics/Marketing Tools at www.demographics.com and follow the link to *American Demographics Magazine.* Review the article entitled "The Age of Self-Navigation" in its September 1996 issue. This article describes changing values in the market segment named "Self-navigators". Information about this consumer segment can help Honda develop products that meet the needs of the college-age market.

What percentage of the US population is in the Self-Navigator segment?

♒

Briefly describe three values held by Self-Navigators.

♒

What cars do Self-Navigators buy?

Competition

How does the CR-V compare with the competition? Prior to finalizing the pricing strategy, you will assist Honda in a competitive analysis. Visit the Honda home page, www.honda.com to find out about the CR-V.

Honda's home page is exceptionally well designed. Notice the graphics and careful organization of topics. This design is consistent with the commercials run by Honda on television. Integrated marketing communication using Web and other media is an important marketing trend.

Now find the Honda CR-V model. When you get to the CR-V page, locate the manufacturer's suggested retail price (MSRP). Write the price and what basic features are included.

Now find *Motor Trend* magazine's home page and click the "search" button. Enter CR-V in the space, and find articles about this automobile. After reviewing the articles identify two competitors for the CR-V.

What are some weaknesses of the CR-V as compared to the competition?

To find out more about the competition, visit the Edmund's automotive home page at www.edmunds.com. Find one competitor you identified above. What is the price range of the competitive model with features similar to those on the CR-V that you priced earlier?

DejaNews

These sites are not the only way for Honda to learn about competition. They can also check the Usenet. The Usenet consists of over 50,000 news groups, each one a forum for public discussion on a very specific topic. People post articles to newsgroups for others to read. Discussions range from the meaningful to the absurd, but marketing planners can learn about products and industries by monitoring discussions. There are even firms that, for a fee, monitor the Usenet and notify corporations of any bad rumors circulating about them. This gives them an opportunity to quickly post a response to dispel the rumor.

We can do some of this sleuthing on our own. A highly specialized search engine called DejaNews has been developed to save and index all postings to the Usenet. So far, DejaNews has indexed over 100 million of these postings and provides a free service which allows you to scan through them.

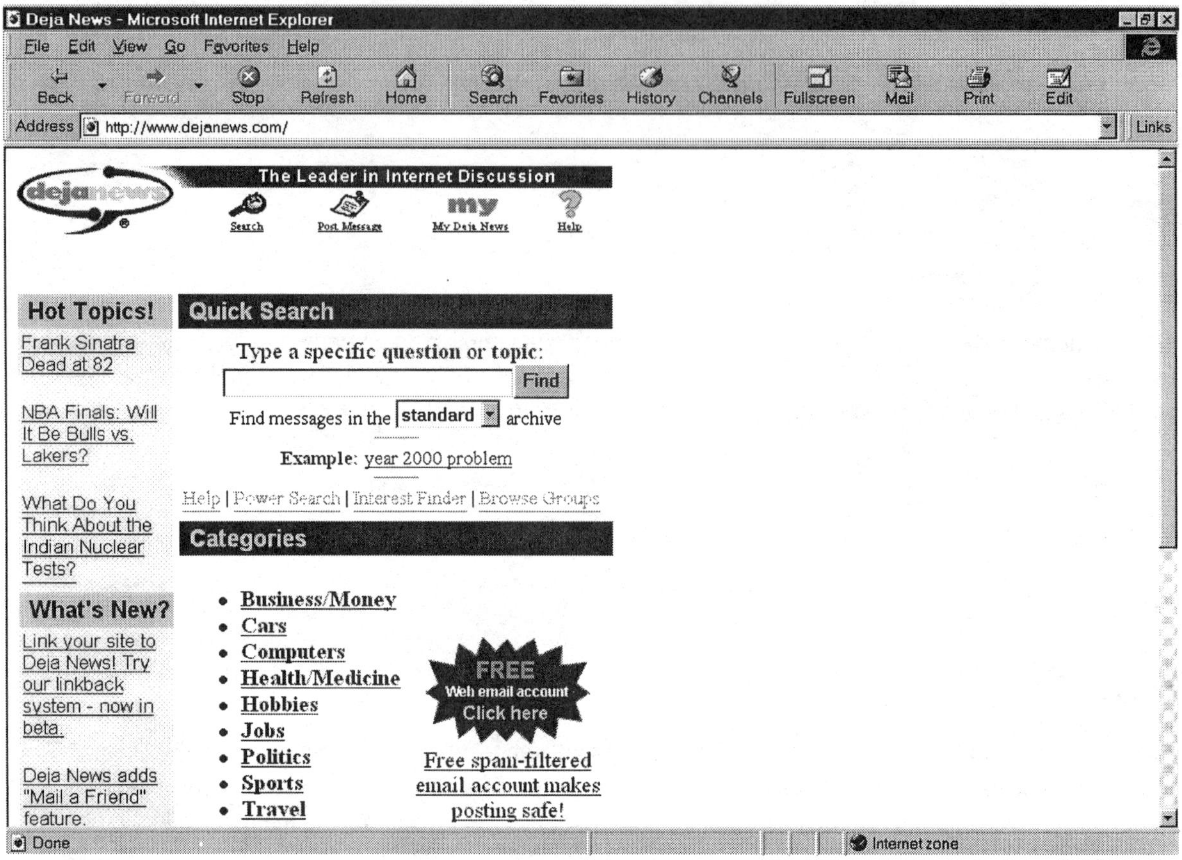

Let's taste the flavor of discussion about the CR-V competition. Visit DejaNews on the Web at www.dejanews.com. Honda would like to know which newsgroups to monitor in the future, so enter one CR-V competitor in the search box then click the Find button. What are four newsgroups you see listed? Note that the ones nearer to the top are rated as more relevant to your search by DejaNews.

Check out some of the conversation and report on one thing that you learn which would be helpful to Honda marketing managers.

How would this information help Honda?

Summary

Now that you have cruised the Web for information about Honda's macroenvironment, we'd like you to make some generalizations about the Net as a source of information. Please answer the following questions in your own words, not with Web addresses.

What is one major Internet source of demographic information for the US market?

What is one place to find data on cultural trends in this country?

In the automobile industry, there are several ways to obtain competitive information. Name two.

Leveraging Technology

Building a Web Site

The process of building and publishing a Web page has become greatly simplified over the last few years. All Web pages rely on the HyperText Markup Language (HTML). HTML uses beginning and end tags to identify which words appear as <B>**Bold**</B>, <I>*Italicized*</I>, <U>Underlined</U>, etc. The tags are placed on either side of the item to be formatted. The end tag begins with a forward slash. The tags are read by the browser (Netscape or Internet Explorer) as page formatting instructions. The user doesn't sees the tags--only the formatted item. If you want to see the tags choose View→HTML Source the next time you are surfing the Web. Programmers actually memorize these tags and use them to construct Web pages. However, many tools generate the tags automatically for you. For example, each product in the Microsoft Office Suite incorporates a "Save as HTML" feature. If you want even more sophisticated Web page design, use a product such as Microsoft FrontPage 98 or NetObjects Fusion. These tools allow non-technical users to design fairly complex Web sites.

Even publishing the pages has become simplified. Transferring files from the designer's computer to the Web server using a procedure called File Transfer Protocol (FTP) publishes web pages. Originally rather cumbersome to use, FTP is now a menu button on FrontPage 98 and Fusion.

The effect of all these design tools will be to spawn a proliferation of Web sites, as they become progressively easy to implement. More businesses will get online and the differences in page design will be minimized. In the future the only point of differentiation between sites will be the content itself. So rule number one for Web sites is to focus on the content!

Chapter 3
Market Analysis Using Primary Data

When secondary data are not available to assist in marketing planning, managers may decide to find their own information. Primary data is information gathered to solve a particular problem. It is usually more expensive and time-consuming to gather than secondary data, but conversely, the data are generally more relevant to the manager's specific problem.

A primary data collection project includes many steps. Briefly, managers must decide the following things:

- What is the exact problem?
- What information is needed to solve the problem?
- Who will provide the information (e.g., consumers)?
- How will managers collect and analyze the data?

Beer at McDonald's

The Problem

Should beer be introduced at US McDonald's locations or not?

The marketing folks at McDonald's may want to introduce beer as a menu item in their restaurants. This could be a risky move because it might upset some families who are a big part of their customer base. On the other hand, beer on the menu might increase McDonald's sales among young singles and other customer groups. Before making this decision, McDonald's would want information about consumer reactions.

Needed Information

Since the US government and other secondary sources do not collect information like this, McDonald's must ask customers themselves. They might make a list of all the **specific information** they need to answer this question. This could include reactions to this new product idea, country and regional differences, and beer brand preferences among McDonald's consumers. Since beer is already on the menu at German McDonald's restaurants, they might want to find out what other consumers are similar to Germans.

Information Providers

They might determine that in order to obtain this information they should ask questions of their current customers in the US, Germany, and other selected countries.

Data Collection

The data collection procedure might include developing a questionnaire and conducting personal interviews in their restaurants during certain time periods. They might even do a beer taste test! Obviously many other decisions will be made concerning such things as sample size, which restaurants to use for interviewing, and data analysis methods.

When companies want to collect primary data from consumers who use the Internet, they often gather this information on the Internet itself. This can be done by sending questionnaires to individuals via e-mail, or by posting a survey on the Web.

Advantages to gathering information online include:

1. It is fast and inexpensive.
2. There is a diverse, large group of Net users all over the world.
3. Consumers often are more frank in their responses because a computer separates them from the folks asking questions.
4. It is novel and many people like filling out questionnaires on the Net.
5. Electronic data are easy to tabulate automatically.

There are many **disadvantages** as well:

1. It is easy for respondents to answer questions untruthfully or to pose as different people (e.g., the opposite sex).
2. People often make more errors typing than they do writing, thus submitting inaccurate information.
3. With Web surveys, there is little control over who or how many people fill out the questionnaire, or whether some people fill it out more than once.

In addition to these disadvantages, there are some **ethical concerns** regarding survey research on the Net:

1. With e-mail surveys, respondents may be upset at getting "junk" e-mail.
2. Some researchers "harvest" e-mail addresses from newsgroups without permission.
3. Some companies conduct "surveys" for the purpose of building a database for later solicitation.

In spite of serious shortcomings, the Net can be a useful place to conduct a primary research project. When using primary or secondary data, you must evaluate its quality carefully and apply it accordingly. In the following exercise you will discover two ways that companies collect primary data about consumers online.

HotWired Online

Learning Objectives

- Experience the Web as a medium for primary data collection
- Explain how e-mail can be used for gathering primary data
- Recognize the advantages and limitations of the Net for primary market research
- Understand some of the privacy issues regarding survey research on the Net

To better understand primary data collection on the Web, we will look at how an online magazine collects data about its subscribers. Wired Digital Inc. controls a number of online services including *HotWired, Wired News, Wired Magazine Online, Ask Dr. Weil, Cocktail, The Rough Guide, HotBot, NewBot, and Suck.* Interestingly, the company that launched the online magazine, *HotWired,* continues to publish its *Wired* magazine on paper. In this exercise, we will visit the *HotWired* online magazine. Like most media, *HotWired's* profits come from selling advertising, not from subscription fees. Anyone with access to the Net can freely access their Web magazine.

Learning About a Firm's Web Customers

Visit *HotWired* at www.hotwired.com. At this site you will see several paid advertisements. Look carefully to find the ads; be sure you are not looking at articles. The ads are generally click-through ads--click on them and you will be transported to the advertiser's web site. One pricing model for online ads is based on the number of users who actually click through. Name the sponsors for two of these ads and briefly describe the market you think they are targeting.

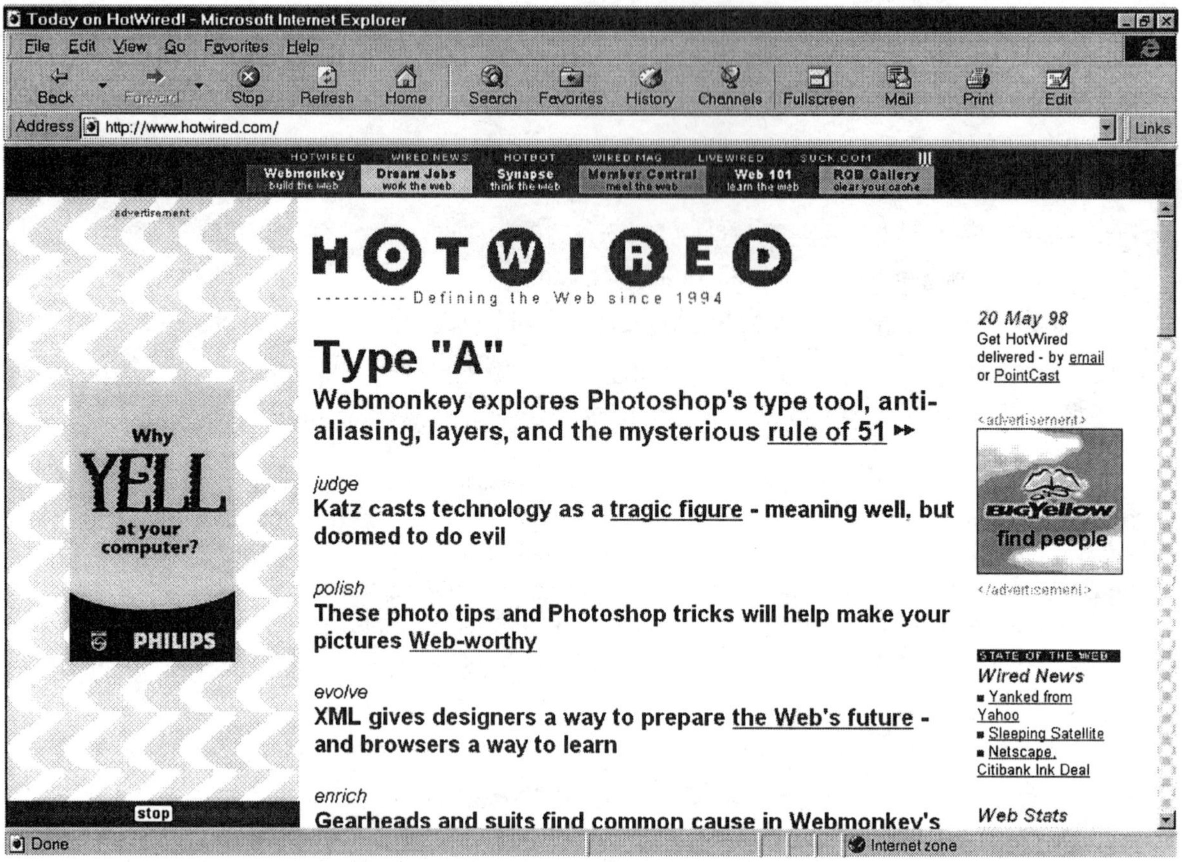

Now become a member by joining the *HotWired* community: "it's free!" While completing the multi page form, answer the following questions.

What are some reasons that *HotWired* wants your e-mail address? Hint: if you gave your e-mail address when registering, you should check your e-mail in-box.

They will ask you to select a unique username. You will use this to sign on each time you visit *HotWired*. From a marketing perspective, why do they want you to do this?

List five things *HotWired* wants to know about you.

HotWired wants to learn about you so they "can better serve the *HotWired* community." How can this personal data help *HotWired* serve you?

How can this information about users help *HotWired* sell more advertising on its Web site?

Privacy Issues

Registration to *HotWired* is optional. One reason for this is that many people will not bother to visit the site if they have to go through the trouble of registering. One reason people don't register at *HotWired* and other sites is privacy. Many users do not want Net firms to have personal information about them. It is a fact, however, that as long as you are connected to another computer via the Internet, your computer sends data to the other computer without your knowledge. This is very similar to "Caller ID" on a telephone. There is a special file on your computer, which other computers are allowed to write to and read data from. This file stores cookies, which are records written by the other computer. When used honestly, cookies are a tremendous benefit to Net commerce. For example, HotWired gave you the option of storing your username and password as a cookie (did you notice?) so that you would not need to sign-on each time you visit. Another application of a cookie is to create an electronic shopping cart that you can fill with items as you shop at a site. Without using cookies it is very difficult for the site to sort out which cart belongs to which visitor. There is a lot of debate in the online community about whether cookies should be banned. There is even a program called CookieCutter which will zap attempts to store cookies on your machine. As a practical matter, however, many sites simply will not support your visit if you don't allow them to write cookies. So for the time being it looks like they are here to stay.

For an example of how some of these items work, go to Yahoo! and search for CDT Privacy. Follow the link and see what is known about you. Depending on the security of your computer network this may be a lot or very little information. Here's what they knew about us:

- **You are affiliated with North American Internet.**
- **Your Internet browser is Microsoft Internet Explorer.**
- **You are coming from hfd-usr3-12.nai.net.**
- **I see you found this page using the yahoo search engine (and I know what you were searching for, too!)**

What do they know about you?

What product does CDT recommend based on this demonstration?

Many sites on the Net don't let you know they are collecting data about you. Do you think it is acceptable for marketers to gather information like this without your knowledge? Why or why not?

New Product Development Through Primary Research

If *HotWired* decided to start another online magazine, it would want to understand what magazines Internet users like to read. *HotWired* might visit DejaNews www.dejanews.com and search for newsgroups discussing **magazines** (you may want to use the "interest finder" feature). When a firm is trying to understand its own customers, this type of observation is a form of primary data collection. Cruise to DejaNews and see what newsgroup *HotWired* might look at and list your recommendation here.

HotWired could also post a questionnaire on the newsgroup and ask for volunteers to respond. What is one question *HotWired* might ask the folks in this group that would help them design a new online magazine?

While at DejaNews, click on the group you recommended. Note that each posting includes the author's e-mail address. *HotWired* could easily copy these addresses and use them to distribute an e-mail questionnaire. This is called harvesting addresses from the Newsgroups, and many firms use this controversial tactic.

Summary

What are the advantages of gathering data about visitors to a company's Web site?

What are the limitations of the data a firm obtains from its Web site?

What are the limitations of the data *HotWired* would get from an e-mail survey using harvested addresses?

What privacy issues are important to marketing researchers on the Net?

Leveraging Technology

Privacy, Log Files and Cookies

Visitors on the Web, like visitors to a sandy beach, leave footprints wherever they go. The footprints are left in two places--on the computer visited and on the user's own computer. The computer visited maintains a log of all computers which visit the site and exactly which pages they see. The log is in the form of a table, which looks similar to this:

Date	Time	Visitor address	Page viewed
9/10/98	10:30am	Frost1.ccsu.edu	Baking recipes
9/10/98	10:31am	Frost1.ccsu.edu	Cookies
9/10/98	10:32am	Frost1.ccsu.edu	Chocolate chip
9/10/98	10:40am	Frost1.ccsu.edu	Sign off

A real log file records much more data. However, even in our simple example you can tell that the computer frost1.ccsu.edu (presumably belonging to Frost at Central Connecticut State University) navigated quickly down to the recipe for chocolate chip cookies and then stayed there for 8 minutes before leaving the site. This type of information collected for thousands of users can tell marketers which pages are popular, who are repeat users, the days and times that the site is most heavily used, etc. Note that the log file only identifies the computer. This makes it difficult to monitor user behavior if more than one user uses the computer.

The second way to track behavior on the Web is by use of cookies. Cookies are files stored on the user's computer. For example suppose you are a repeat visitor to a site which requires a password. The site could authenticate you by looking up your password in a cookie file stored on your computer. They could also use the cookie file to store your purchase choices in an electronic shopping basket prior to checkout. One textbook publisher sells cookies to students so they can access the online textbook materials.

Both log files and cookies can be positively used to help customize products and services to the user community. However, most users do not understand how their behavior is being tracked and this raises a serious question. Is it ethical to gather information about people without their knowledge and explicit consent?

Chapter 4

Audience Characteristics and Behavior

In April 1998, the total number of people twelve and older using the Internet was greater than 57 million (source: www.relevantknowledge.com). It is no wonder that the number of businesses displaying their wares on the Web is also growing. Before rushing to put a page on the Web, however, companies must attempt to understand the characteristics and Net behavior of those 57 million Net users. Armed with this information, companies can determine if their target markets are in the Net audience, and can further decide how to develop Web sites that attract and appeal to potential customers.

What specific information do organizations want to know about the audience for this medium?

- Size and growth trend
- Demographics
- Geographic location of computer
- Psychographics
- Behavior on the Net

Size

Will the Internet's phenomenal growth rate continue? When television was first introduced, most believed it would grow as a channel of communication. Few predicted that it would be the fastest growing advertising medium in the history of the US. Will the Internet continue to grow until it assumes the power of television? Or will it settle as a smaller niche medium, following the prediction of cybercritics? Before investing substantial time and money on maintaining an Internet presence, companies need answers to these questions.

Demographics

Demographics include such things as age, income and ethnicity. Knowledge of Net audience demographics can aid an organization in determining whether its target markets are online. Where can Net user demographics be found? The US Census Web site provides demographics for the entire population, but not the segment frequenting the Net. Individual Web sites such as *HotWired* collect information from those who are willing to fill out registration forms. This information is helpful, but far from a complete description of all users. It is also proprietary to the company collecting it. The fastest and least expensive source of information about Net user demographics is from research firms that conduct surveys and report results on the Web itself. Several firms provide demographic data, but as the mainstream population adopts the Internet, user composition continues to change rapidly. Also, as mentioned in Chapter 3, there are many limitations to primary data that are collected online. There is much controversy over who exactly is "out there."

Geographics

Although the geographic location of computers in cyberspace is not important to users, it is important to companies wanting to be on the Web. The first reason for this is that a company may not wish to distribute its products to the entire planet. If a company only wants to serve France, for example, it will want to know how many Net users are in that location. In fact, there are an increasing number of Web sites that serve only local users. Second, the geographic distribution of users has language implications. Most Net text is currently in the English language. Companies wanting to serve countries that do not speak English may want to create Web pages in other languages. If you visit the Bayer site (the aspirin manufacturer), you will see that the home page offers users a choice of English or German.

Psychographics

User psychographics include personality, lifestyle, and activities, interests and opinions (AIO). This information can also assist in target market matching, but is especially important to Web page design. For example, if we think that most Web users are upwardly mobile, we might create pages that appeal to the desire for luxury and success. There is an increasing amount of psychographic information available on the Web about Net users.

Behavior

User behavior on the Net is of vital importance to marketers. Companies want to know how much time people spend on the Net, what they do while they are there, how they learn about new Web sites, and whether or not they buy merchandise on the Web. Web advertisers also want to know whether Net users also watch TV, listen to the radio, or read newspapers and magazines. This information will help advertisers decide how to allocate their budgets among various media.

Finding Answers

Fortunately, much of this information about Net users is available as secondary data. Statistics are reported in traditional media as well as on the Web itself. Businesses can also purchase high quality secondary data from market research firms such as A. C. Nielsen and FIND/SVP. In the following exercise, you will do some exploring in order to build a profile of Net user characteristics and behavior using free online secondary data.

CyberAtlas Planning a Zine

Learning Objectives

- Use secondary data to describe the Net audience
- Explore sites that have conducted surveys of Net users
- Apply information about Net users to create a Web magazine

How big is the Internet, really? This question has no easy answer. For this exercise, you will review several surveys of Internet users to understand the market size and its demographics, geographics, psychographics and Net behavior. You will then use this information to help determine the potential market for a "Zine," a Web magazine. You will need to determine both the types of articles to include and the kind of products or services that should be advertised based on their appeal to the Web audience.

Why does each survey give a different answer about the size, composition, and behavior of the Net audience? This is a problem inherent in survey research methodolgy, and is particularly problematic for research conducted online. It is difficult to obtain a random sample of the population and survey participants do not always answer honestly. Because the possibility for error is so great, market researchers tend to be very critical of survey methodology. Much of the information you will review in this exercise has been subject to criticism--but it is the best that we have. The Nielsen TV ratings are always criticized as well, but they are still widely used.

One sticking point is defining who counts as a Net user. For example, if you have a computer in your home that connects to the Internet are you a Net user? What if you've used it once in the last six months? How about once in the last week? Should we count only regular users? You can begin to see the problem.

CyberAtlas

We will assume you are constructing a magazine with the broadest market appeal. Therefore, you need to develop a profile of the typical Web user. CyberAtlas has done a nice job of compiling research findings from various organizations. They even offer links back to the organizations referenced on their site. Go to CyberAtlas at www.cyberatlas.com to complete the sections that follow.

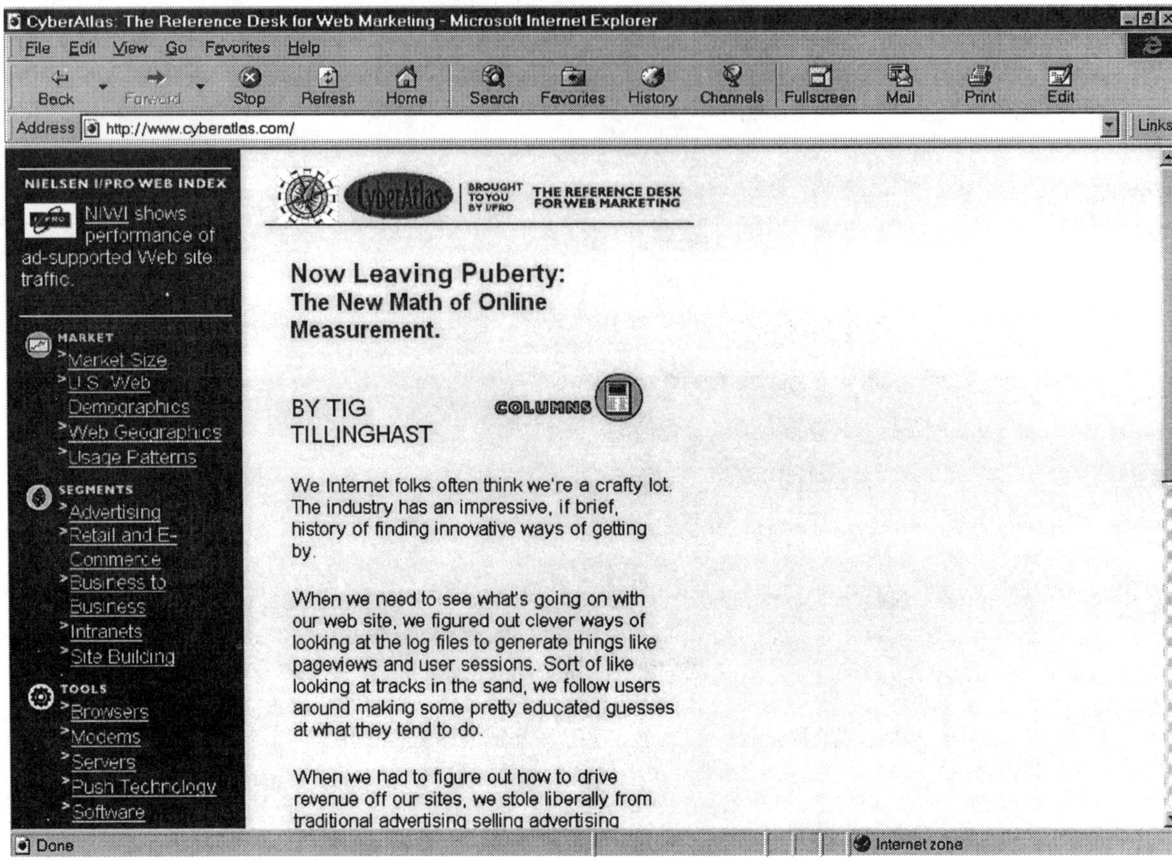

Market Size

Users

Your magazine will be distributed on the Web so you need to know how many folks are "out there." This number is hard to verify, but many firms make estimates. How many people use the Web?

Millions of People	Source	Date

Demographics

Gender

Is the typical Web user male or female?

Gender	%	Source	Date
Male			
Female			

Age

In order to reach about 50% of Web users, what age ranges would you target?

Age Range	%	Source	Date

Education

In order to reach about 50% of Web users, what education levels would you target?

Education Level	%	Source	Date

Income

What income levels should you target?

Income Level	%	Source	Date

Occupation

What occupations should you target?

Occupation	%	Source	Date

User Behavior

Activities

What are the top five Internet activities enjoyed by users?

Activity	% Enjoying	Source

Geographics

In the past of couple years, the number of users from countries other than North America and Western Europe has grown considerably. Other than North America and Western Europe, what two countries or regions appear to have the best potential for your Zine?

Country or Region	Statistic as Evidence	Source

Stanford Research Institute (SRI) iVALS

SRI's Values and Lifestyles Program (VALS) is used by many marketers who wish to understand the psychographics of both existing and potential customers. SRI categorizes people by two dimensions: self-identity and resources. The philosophy is that consumers purchase products that shape their identities using psychological, physical, demographic and material resources. SRI developed a series of questionnaires to measure these attributes and then placed respondents in lifestyle groups. As a companion to VALS, SRI developed Internet VALS (iVALS) to describe the values and lifestyles of Internet users. Since we are targeting Internet users we will use the iVALS survey. Information about Web user psychographics will help plan your new magazine.

Visit SRI at future.sri.com and follow links to the iVALS questionnaire. Take the iVALS survey and list your type here.

Briefly describe the Net behavior of your iVALS type.

If you were targeting the iVALS Mainstreamers, what product advertising you would seek for your new magazine?

Summary and Analysis

Describe a typical Web user (demographic profile).

Based on what you learned about Internet users, what content area and appeal would you choose for your magazine?

Produce a title for your magazine:

Write titles for two articles you'd include in your new magazine based on this information.

What products and services might you advertise in your magazine?

Leveraging Technology

Audience Measurement

Measuring Web site traffic has become a big business precisely because it is difficult to do well. Advertisers demand accurate and verifiable measures before they will pay for ads on sites. Rarely are they willing to accept the claims of the sites themselves--rather the advertisers seek out the services of third party measurement firms. These third party services will audit the log file of the Web site. They take a sample from the log file and then generate usage statistics. The process is similar to auditing the subscription list for a magazine. However, the measurement companies have known for some time that the readership is always greater than the subscription list. Why? Because multiple readers view each issue. For example, many people read magazines in doctors' offices and health clubs. As a result magazine companies conduct readership surveys to estimate this "pass along" readership. The Web has a similar problem. Many organizations actually make copies of Web sites and then let their employees access the copies. This is done to speed access since a local copy will load far faster than one pulled off of the Internet. The process is accomplished by use of a proxy server, which keeps the copy at the corporate site. The problem however is that the original site now has no record of visits to the proxy server. And unfortunately for Web sites there are no agreed upon standards for audience multipliers--though some studies indicate that as much as 70% of the readership is not counted. Consequently, one measurement company, Match Logic, has begun to count this readership in a clever way. While they allow the Web site to be copied or cached by proxy servers, they do not allow the ads to be similarly cached. In fact they don't store ads permanently on the Web page. Instead they program the Web page itself to request a new ad from Match Logic's ad server every time that it is viewed. The ad server counts the requests and the measurement problem is solved.

Chapter 5
The Net for Product Planning

A product is something that satisfies the needs of organizations or consumers and for which they are willing to exchange money or other items of value. Products can be tangible items, intangible services, people, ideas, places, or any combination of these things.

Is the Internet a Product?

From one perspective, the Internet is a channel of communication, similar to a magazine, television, or a direct mail letter. Content providers and the Net audience send information back and forth over it. From a technological viewpoint, the Internet is a network of computers. Because "Internet" is a general term that encompasses many different functions, the Internet itself is not a product. However, a great number of new products have emerged to meet the needs of Internet users. Examples of truly innovative products are search engines such as Yahoo!, software to develop Web pages, services that audit the traffic at Web sites, and a whole list of new technologies such as cable modems. Taking a less risky step, some companies use the Internet to extend their current brands: examples include online stock brokerage services and newspaper publishing. New product opportunities exist in many areas from information and product delivery to the Net's technology infrastructure and the computers or televisions used to access the Internet.

The Internet for Product Planning

The Internet is a resource for gathering information about competitors, patents, consumers, and other environmental issues that aid in product planning. In previous exercises, you used the Internet to gather information, evaluate consumer data and to plan a new magazine. Since you have already had extensive experience with product planning on the Net, we can focus on one small aspect of the product function: brand naming and trademarks.

Brand Names and Trademarks

A brand is a name, (McDonald's), a symbol (golden arches), or other identifying information. When a firm registers that information with the US Patent office, it becomes a trademark, and thus is legally protected from imitation. According to the US government, "a trademark is either a word, phrase, symbol or design, or combination of words, phrases, symbols or designs, which identifies and distinguishes the source of the goods or services of one party from those of others" (source: www.uspto.gov).

Organizations spend a lot of time and money developing strong, unique brand names. Using the company trademark in the Web address helps consumers quickly find the site. For example, www.coca-cola.com adds power to Coca-Cola brands. In the following exercise, you will discover how companies obtain domain names for their Web pages.

The Internet and Trademarks

Learning Objectives

- Understand what part of a Web address can be legally "owned" by an organization
- Learn how to register a domain name

It is not unusual in business for corporations in completely different industries to share part of the same brand name (e.g., Apple Computer and Apple Records). However, if you search for www.apple.com which company would you expect to see? Most would expect the computer company and indeed that is what shows up. What about a search for www.delta.com? Would you expect the airline? The faucet company? Wrong on both counts. DeltaComm, a software developer and Internet Service Provider in North Carolina was the first to register www.delta.com--so it belongs to them. Use Yahoo! to find the addresses for Delta Airlines and Delta Faucet.

Company	Web Address
DeltaComm	
Delta Airlines	
Delta Faucet	

InterNIC

Fortunately the Internet community has an organization called the InterNIC with which companies can register their domain names. The agency also tries to mediate disputes and avoid getting sued in the process (not always successfully). In this exercise you will choose a name for the Web Zine which you prepared in a previous exercise and begin the actual process of registering your name on InterNIC's server. Please do not complete the registration process unless you really want to own (and pay for) that name.

Begin by selecting three names that you would consider original and catchy for your Zine.

-
-
-

Now sign on to InterNIC's site at www.internic.net. (Note: since InterNIC is a network organization it is found under the **net** domain).

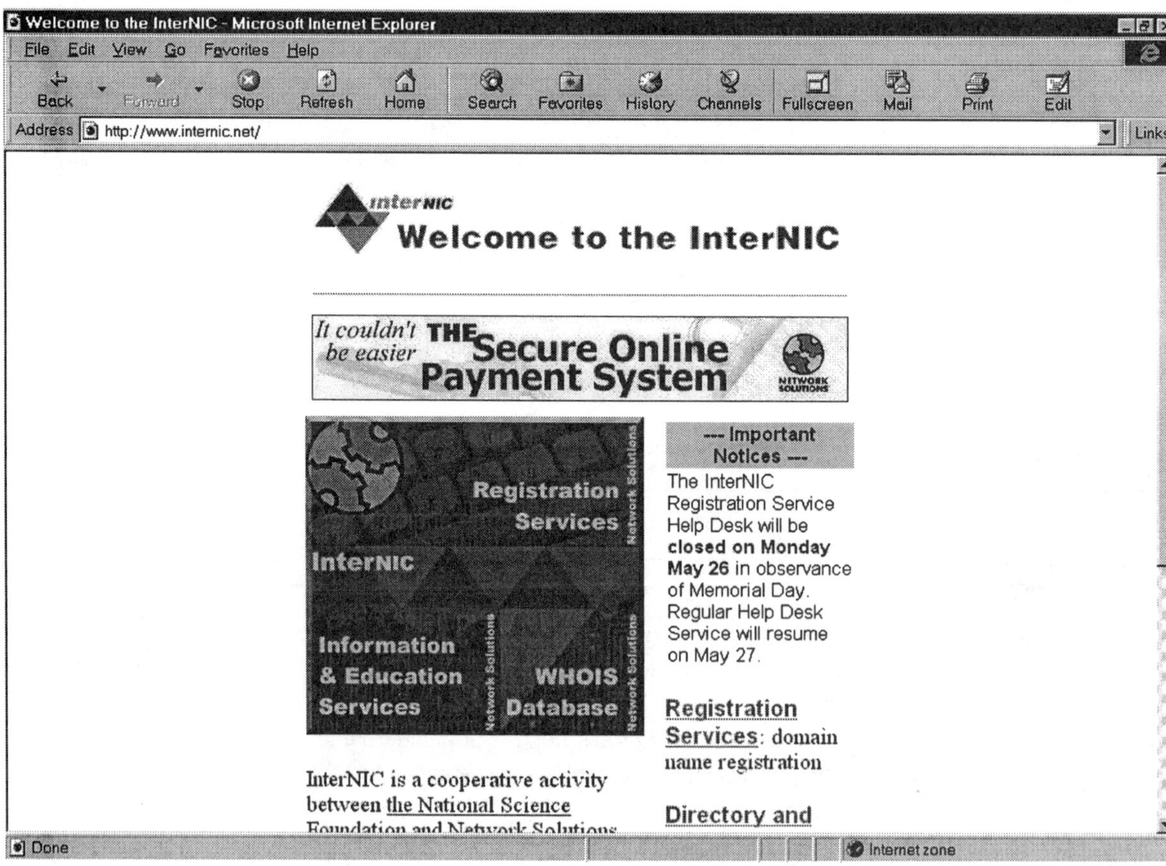

Like brand names, once a domain name is taken, it is not available to others. InterNIC's WHOIS Database engine will tell us which names are registered, when they were registered and who registered the name.

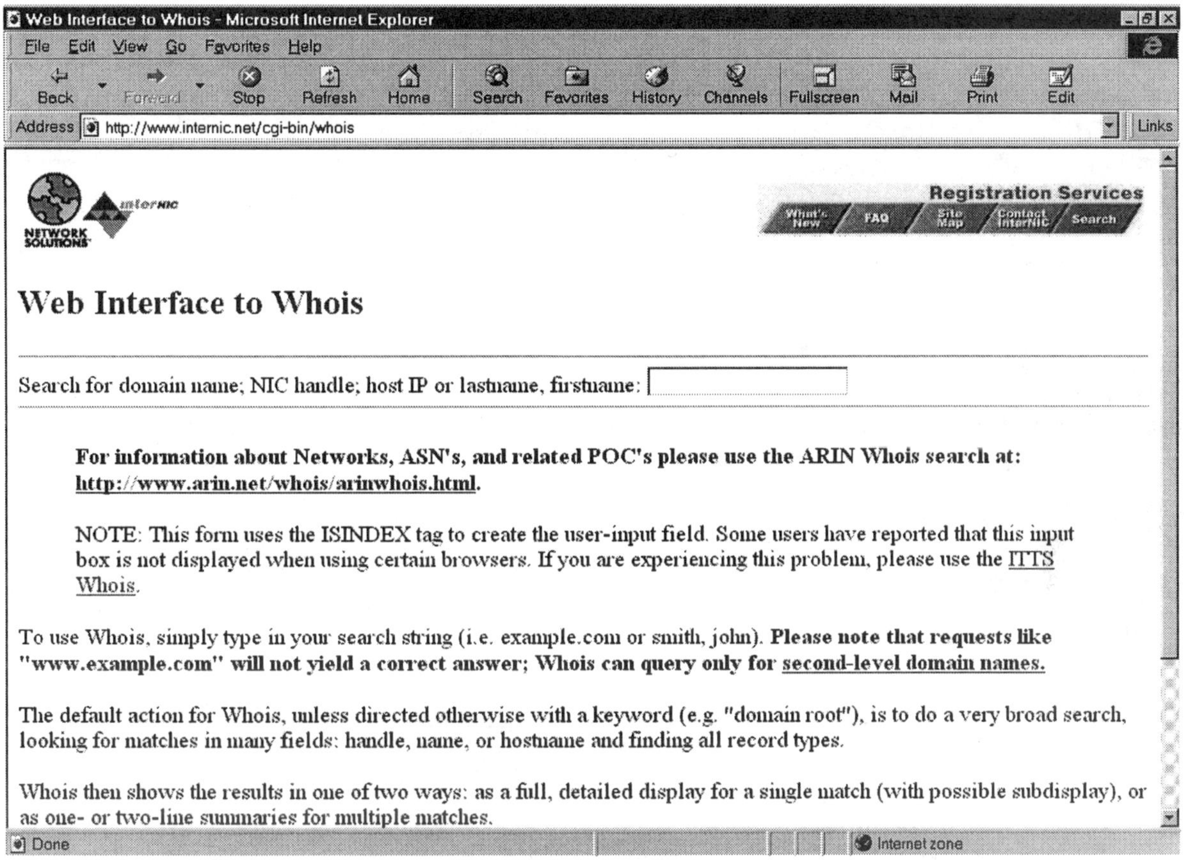

For the following domains use WHOIS to see when they first registered their name (the record created date). Do not include the WWW in your search string. Type coca-cola.com not www.coca-cola.com.

Domain Name	Date First Registered
Coca-cola.com	14-Oct-94
Odci.gov	
Delta.com	
Delta-air.com	
Deltafaucet.com	
Your University (e.g., ccsu.edu)	

Now check to see if your catchy Zine names are registered and if so who owns them.

Your Catchy Zine Domain Names	Who Owns It?

Find the registration forms on the interNIC site. Locate the domain name registration form, and then follow the link for the Web version of the form. This is the real form and if you fill it out you may end up with a real bill. How much money will the name cost you? The answer is on this form and on the registration information page.

Don't have that kind of cash handy? Use the back button on your browser to return to the home page.

Summary

Why does an organization want to use its trademark or a brand name in the address for its Web site?

What could a company do if its brand name is already registered to someone else as a domain name?

Do you think that InterNIC should charge for domain names? Why or why not?

Some companies buy hundreds of domain names that they then redistribute (e.g., www.bestdomains.com). Why would they do this?

Do you think it is right for companies like Bestdomains to buy domain names for brands they don't own?

Leveraging Technology

DNS Servers

When you register a domain name you will also be assigned an Internet Protocol (IP) address. For example the domain name for Central Connecticut State University is www.ccsu.edu. The IP address, which corresponds to this domain name, is 149.152.125.2. Typing either the domain name or the IP address into the browser would take you to CCSU's homepage. However people have a hard time remembering IP addresses and find it much easier to remember the domain name. The Internet Service Provider (ISP) must therefore dedicate a computer called a (Domain Name Server) DNS to translate domain names to IP addresses. The server maintains a table to do the translation that looks something like this:

Domain Name	IP Address
www.ccsu.edu	149.152.125.2
www.mcdonalds.com	204.152.144.180
Guess who? Try it and see	204.71.200.69

Sometimes you will get an error message when you search for a site that the domain name was not found. This means that the DNS server has no entry for the address. Either you typed the address incorrectly or the DNS server has not updated its table to add the entry you are seeking. When an organization upgrades its Web server to a new machine, they will simply assign the IP address to the new machine and then users will immediately be able to access it.

Chapter 6

The Net as a Distribution Channel

Prior to this chapter, we presented the Net as a tool for marketing planning. Marketers use the Net for primary and secondary research, which aids in decision making. In this chapter, we introduce the Net as part of the marketing mix: it is a distribution channel (the "place" component of the four P's). First, we'll review the distribution function, then explain how the Net aids marketers with product distribution.

What is a Distribution Channel?

A distribution channel is a set of firms and individuals that facilitate the movement of product from producer to business user or consumer. Many companies use marketing intermediaries, such as wholesalers, between them and the consumer. These intermediaries often take ownership of the product and resell it to other intermediaries along the channel. This type of channel is called an **indirect** distribution channel. A typical indirect channel includes a manufacturer, wholesaler, retailer, and consumer. If no intermediaries are used, the channel is **direct**: product flows directly from producer to consumer or business user.

In many cases the Internet eliminates intermediaries from the channel. For example, the manufacturer may sell directly to consumers. This results in lower costs to consumers and/or higher margins for the manufacturer. On a less positive note, disintermediation also results in a loss of jobs. In some cases the Internet has spawned new intermediaries. For example, shopping agents assist Internet users in finding the right product at the lowest price.

The Net and Distribution

Direct Channel

The Net has emerged as part of a firm's distribution channel in two ways. First, the Net is a complete direct channel: digital products are sent from producer to user directly over the Net. Digital products available on the Net are software, audio, video, graphics, and text. Hundreds of radio stations broadcast live over the Net in many different languages, and users with appropriate software (e.g., RealPlayer from RealNetworks www.real.com) can listen in real time. This is an example of product delivery over the Net. The same is true for live video using the same software. These two uses of the Net are still in early stages of development and are expected to grow in the future. The major barrier to these products is lack of bandwidth. Even the fastest modems at 50,000 bits per second are just too slow. Low bandwidth results in choppy and grainy audio and video communication. Fortunately, text and still graphics are not so time sensitive and therefore can be delivered over a low bandwidth channel. There are many magazines that now have online e-Zine versions, and many newspapers deliver their product via the Net as well. You explored *HotWired* in an earlier chapter, and you will review the *New York Times* online in this chapter.

Indirect Channel

The Web also serves as an electronic retailer in indirect distribution channels. There are many electronic storefronts and virtual malls in cyberspace, and an increasing number of Net users are patronizing these retailers. Users can shop in virtual stores and order product directly over the Net. According to Cyberatlas.com, in 1997 40% of all companies with Web sites engaged in electronic commerce: some of the most sought after products were financial services, travel, music, books, and automobiles. Our experiences shopping on the Web have all been positive.

Transaction Security

Transaction security is one of the problems associated with Net retailing and direct distribution. When a product is purchased, there must be a way for users to pay instantaneously for fast delivery. Many users are hesitant to give their credit card number over the Net out of fear that it will be stolen. Tremendous strides have been made in data encryption to prevent this type of theft but some users remain skeptical. We suspect that the fear will diminish as the technology becomes more familiar. Fearful users at one time even shunned ATM machines.

Encryption protects the transaction while it is in transit between your computer and the retailer. Sometimes, however, the retailer does not adequately protect the records stored on their computer. In one security breach, the online storefronts of ESPN SportsZone and NBA.com were "broken into." The hacker stole the credit card numbers and e-mail addresses of hundreds of customers. As proof, he then sent each person e-mail containing their card number.

One of the best ways to protect against this type of break in is to hire a professional to try to break into your computer system. They are able to recognize flaws in the security system of your computer and suggest remedies to make it more secure. There are even computer programs such as Smurf, PingOdeath, and Satan Scan that you can use to attack your own site. And of course there are corresponding intrusion detection systems such as Real Secure and Entrust to notify you of an actual attack by recognizing the digital signatures of these attack programs.

Music Boulevard

Learning Objectives

- Understand the Net as a direct distribution channel
- Explain the Net as electronic retailer in the distribution channel
- Differentiate uniform delivered pricing and zone delivered pricing for Net retailers

Online retailing is a growing industry on the Net. There are thousands of virtual storefronts offering their wares. It is not always easy to distinguish between a large, well-established operation and a new one based in a garage. Fortunately, there are services that describe other online services. In this exercise, we will explore one of those services and visit one of the top online music stores.

First connect to Yahoo!. Select shopping from the Yahoo! services. At the shopping page, choose the category "music." Bookmark this page: you might want to return to compare prices! When you visit the music merchants represented at Yahoo! you'll see a listing of various online music stores. Music Boulevard has an extremely large inventory, so let's visit.

What promotions are they offering?

♒

Now let's see what's on sale. From the main screen click on either a "specials" or "on sale" button. Surf in your favorite category and list three albums that are on sale.

ARTIST	Album Title	Price

Using the Search feature, look for **Will Smith** (artist name).

If you have RealPlayer installed on your computer, you can click on the audio button next to an album and listen to short samples from selected tracks!

Click on the buy button next to one of their albums to put it in your "shopping basket" (you will dump it later). Press the continue to shop button and repeat the exercise for one other artist of your choice. You should now have two items in your shopping basket. Complete the following table by 1) recording the contents of your shopping basket, and 2) writing the subtotal of your bill (before taxes and shipping and handling).

ARTIST	Album Title	Price
Will Smith		
SUBTOTAL		

Find the shipping and handling charges from Music Boulevard in order to have the two CDs shipped by the Postal Service within the US.

Music Boulevard offers several different pricing strategies for shipping. **Uniform delivered shipping** (postage stamp pricing) is when the delivery price is the same for all customers, regardless of residential location. **Zone delivered pricing** is when the manufacturer divides the country into zones and charges a different amount depending on location. What type of pricing scheme does Music Boulevard use for its domestic customers (try looking in the help menu)?

What is the delivery charge to have the two CDs sent via airmail to the Bahamas?

What pricing strategy is Music Boulevard using for international customers?

Why do you think the two pricing strategies differ?

Now back up and empty your shopping basket by clicking the delete button next to each item on your bill. Press recalculate and your basket will be emptied.

Just for fun you might want to return to Yahoo! shopping services and see if you can find these albums for less elsewhere.

The Net as a Direct Channel for Distributing Product

NY Times

In the previous exercise we looked at an online store which distributes its products via traditional methods. We foresee a day when the music will be transported over the Internet link and then burned onto a CD stored on your computer. The major obstacle to this today is that music files are enormous and there is not enough bandwidth on most connections to download the music in a reasonable period of time. However the same is not true of text and graphics. We have enough bandwidth today to free the text and graphics from paper and transport them directly to the desktop. In this exercise we will look at the Net as a direct channel for distributing product. Only digital products such as software, newspapers, and magazines can be directly distributed or sent over a communication channel.

Find the *NY Times* on the Web. What is their address?

Choose the option to Tour the Site, taking the guided quick tour. Record ten of the pages you visit and provide a one-sentence description of each.

Page	Description

Reviewing all offered sections, which ones, if any, differ from a regular newspaper?

♒

Go back to the home page. Visit the help center and look up pricing. What does the *NY Times* charge domestic users of this service?

♒

The NYT charges a fee for some of its digital product. What are these services and what is the fee?

♒

Now visit the *Wall Street Journal's* site at www.wsj.com. What does the *WSJ* charge users of their online paper?

♒

Speculate as to why the subscription fees for the *NY Times* and the *Wall Street Journal* differ.

♒

One reason we chose the *NY Times* site is because of a clever feature they have implemented in conjunction with Netscape. The feature offers to send you Web pages on a daily basis with news customized to meet your needs. What's interesting about the feature is that the pages are e-mailed to you. This follows the push model of distribution as opposed to the pull model so common to the Web. You don't have to visit the Web page; the page comes directly to your browser.

Netscape's motivation in this venture is obvious. The service only works if you are using the Netscape Navigator browser (version 3.0 or better). The *Times'* motivation is subject to speculation. They expose you to the *Times* (and their advertisers) on a daily basis, thus building brand loyalty. Also, we might hypothesize that they can use this service to lighten peak load on their server by distributing the news at off-peak hours.

Summary

Explain the Internet as direct distribution channel.

♒

What function does the Net serve as a marketing intermediary in an indirect distribution channel?

♒

By filling out online order forms for products, you save the distributor a significant operating cost--what is it?

♒

How are online newspapers different from regular newspapers?

♒

Leveraging Technology

Site Rating Services

As sites proliferate it will become increasingly difficult for consumers to distinguish between reputable and non-reputable sites. Consumers will increasingly need to rely on reference services to select retail products and services. One rating service, Bizrate, is particularly interesting. Web sites agree to let Bizrate randomly sample their customer base. They are like the J. D. Powers of the Web. The cumulative responses along different dimensions are then published on the Bizrate site. The dimensions include:

Pre-purchase

- Price
- Product
- Selection
- Product
- Information
- Web site
- Aesthetics
- Web site
- Navigation

Post-purchase

- On-time Delivery
- Product
- Availability
- (In-Stock)
- Customer Support
- Ease of Returns
- Customer Loyalty

Additionally Bizrate indicates the availability of the following services on each site.

- Secure ordering/payment system (SSL/SET)
- Online ordering shopping chart system
- Online order tracking system
- Customer information privacy
- Gift wrapping
- Live customer support
- International shipping
- Product search

While they accept no advertising or sponsorship, they make their money buy selling detailed copies of the reports back to the merchants. These include trends over time along each dimension.

Chapter 7

The Net as a Marketing Communication Medium

The Net is an important marketing communication vehicle for marketers. Organizations promote to various audiences through advertising, public relations, sales promotion and personal selling. Currently, the Web's biggest uses are advertising and public relations, though this is changing.

Advertising

For marketers, the Net is similar to a magazine or a television. These media have content (i.e., articles and programs) and they sell advertising. Some content providers offer classified advertising to Net users. Other content providers, who are especially successful at drawing large audiences, sell designated advertising space on their Web pages. These ads are called banners and buttons. You have already visited *HotWired* and seen ads on their pages. You also may have noticed banner ads whenever you search the Web using Yahoo or AltaVista. Sponsorships are another type of Web advertising. On television, the Hallmark Hall of Fame is an example of a program (content) sponsorship. On the Web, a company such as Kraft, develops recipe content and pays to place it on a Web site targeted to homemakers. The only way a user can tell Kraft paid for the sponsorship is to look for logos or mentions of Kraft brands on the page.

Web advertising is in an interesting, developmental stage. At this point, there are no perfect ways to measure the number of people who visit a page. Thus, it is difficult for advertisers to know how much to pay for an ad, or even to know whether the ad is effective. New measurement techniques are becoming more sophisticated as the amount of money invested in Web advertising continues to grow.

One sophisticated advertising technique used by some of the search engines is to target the banner ads to the search terms that you type in. For example, if you type Toyota as a search term, you would see ads for Toyota car dealerships.

Public Relations

The Web is an important vehicle for public relations activities. PR creates goodwill among an organization's stakeholders. It is important for a company to communicate with customers, employees, the government, the media, shareholders, and many other groups in order to influence public opinion. PR communication tools include special events, publicity through press releases, public service campaigns, and publications such as newsletters, brochures and annual reports. The term "brochureware" emerged to define Web sites that contain only product or company information. On the Web, companies use PR in some of the following ways:

- Direct communication with consumers via e-mail or Web forms
- Online special events, such as the Microsoft Windows '95 anniversary party
- Online information for various publics, such as product information and annual reports
- Electronic press releases for PR publicity

Sales Promotions

Sales promotions are short-term incentives that aid the movement of product from producer to consumer. Some sales promotion tactics directed at consumers include coupons, rebates, premiums, contests and sweepstakes. Most of these are currently offered on the Web. For example, Coupons Online (www.couponsonline.com) and Hot Coupons (www.hotcoupons.com) provide electronic coupons on the Web. Consumers print them or have them sent to their homes. The Rollerblade exercise gives you a chance to enter a sweepstakes of your choice.

Personal Selling

The Net is not used for personal selling because the computer mediates communication between audience and content provider: it is impersonal. The Net is used to generate leads for salespeople, however. For example, Herman Miller, producer of office furniture, sells most of its products to businesses. A visit to their Web site (www.hermanmiller.com) offers users a chance to complete the "guest book," and request contact from a salesperson: "I'm ready to buy one of your products or services. Please have a Herman Miller salesperson contact me."

Push and Pull Promotional Strategies

"Pull" promotional strategies are those directed to the ultimate consumer. Tools such as advertising and coupons entice consumers to seek out retailers in search of a product, pulling it from the distribution channel. "Push" strategies are normally directed to resellers within the channel. Tactics such as price discounts encourage wholesalers and retailers to buy products, enabling producers to push product down the channel. Most marketing communication on the Net currently follows the pull model. Promotions directed to consumers entice them to visit Web sites. Users surf the Net to find information and entertainment: they pull pages to their desktops. Recently, some firms are beginning to push information to user computers. For example, the *New York Times* offers a service whereby readers can request that particular sections of the newspaper be sent to them via e-mail. Also, Pointcast, USA Today and Time Warner offer free computer screen savers that automatically bring news and ads to your desktop. Television currently uses a push model of information communication, and many predict that the Web will eventually be delivered similarly.

Marketing Communications at Rollerblade

Learning Objectives

- Understand Web sites as electronic brochures
- Describe how Web sites can be used for two-way communication with customers
- Discuss the use of Web sites for communicating about PR special events, sponsorships, and public service campaigns
- Discover places to send electronic press releases announcing new Web sites
- Evaluate alternative Web pages for online advertising
- Tell how the Web can be used for sales promotions

Rollerblade makes in-line skates. Of course, you already knew that. Their success has had a lot to do with their hot products and much to do with their savvy marketing promotions. In this exercise we look at their online promotional techniques, evaluating Rollerblade's PR and sales promotion techniques, and discovering online advertising opportunities for them. Visit Rollerblade at www.rollerblade.com.

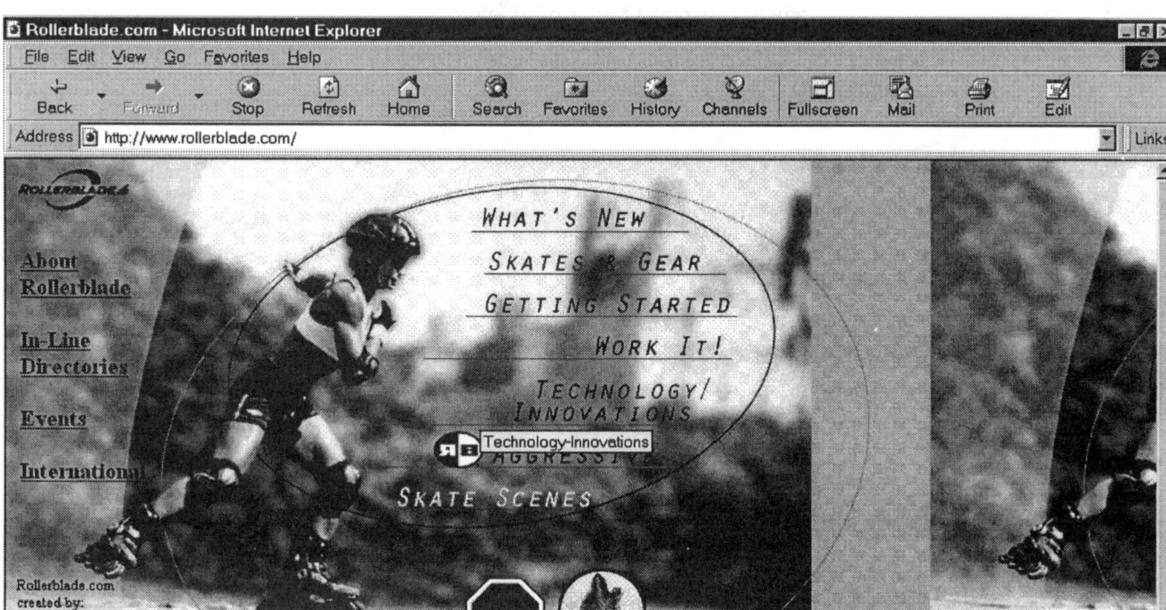

Public Relations

Rollerblade's web site is a good example of how sites can be used for public relations. First, the site itself is a PR tool, similar to a product brochure. Second, it develops good customer relations by helping customers through the maze of product options. Look for a page that lists various skates on Rollerblade's site and follow links based on your skating needs. Which Rollerblade skate is best for you?

As part of their PR, Rollerblade sponsors an in-line skate racing team. Can you find the name of this team on the Rollerblade site?

From the site home page, visit What's New and describe one PR special event that you find there.

An important aspect of public relations is the customer's ability to talk with the company. How does Rollerblade provide for feedback?

Press Releases

What should Rollerblade do to publicize its Web site? One easy way to advertise the address for a Web site is to put it on all product packaging and promotion. Another way is to ask related sites to provide free links to its page. Name one Web site that might want to link to Rollerblade as a service to its audience.

A final PR step involves sending press releases to the search engines, and many other places known for free Web site listing. For a summary of how to publicize a Web site, visit www.submit-it.com. After reviewing their free information on how to publicize a site (Web site marketing primer), list and briefly describe seven major ways to publicize the new Rollerblade Web site.

Method	Description

Note that Submit-it will do all the work of publicizing your site if you are willing to pay them. Some of the services like Submit-it claim to be able to have your site listed in the first screen that appears when a Web user queries for a related term using a search engine.

Advertising

Rollerblade may even pay others to provide a link to its home page. These links are most often in the form of banner ads which the user can click-through to visit the advertised site. To help Rollerblade, let's evaluate three sites that sell advertising space. Visit www.adhome.com and complete the following table for ESPN and two other appropriate sites. Note that sites which compile lists of advertisers are usually short lived. If Adhome is not operative when you complete this exercise, simply go directly to a few sports sites or search engines and see if you can find their rates to complete the table.

Site	Package	Monthly Cost	Guaranteed Impressions per Month	Cost per 1000 impressions $CPM = \frac{cost}{impressions} * 1000$
ESPNET SportsZone				

Taking into account price (efficiency) and relevant target audience coverage (effectiveness), what is your recommendation for Rollerblade's advertising and why?

≈

Sales Promotion

Contests, sweepstakes and games are popping up all over the Web. They build excitement about brands, and can encourage purchase. More specific to the Web, they draw the audience to a site and keep them returning. Sweepstakes are pure luck of the draw. Sponsors cannot require a purchase because then the sales promotion is considered a lottery and would be covered under gambling law. Conversely, contests require skill, such as correctly answering a trivia question.

Visit the games and giveaways page at www.playhere.com/giveaway.htm In their sweepstakes section find a prize that is appealing to you. Follow the link to the site sponsoring the sweepstakes. What is the Web address and company name for the site sponsoring this sweepstakes?

≈

What is the first prize (the one that drew YOU to this page)?

≈

What marketing purpose do you think this organization has for running the sweepstakes?

Summary

What are 4 ways an organization can use its Web site for PR purposes?

Why do advertisers use CPM to evaluate advertising costs?

What are two popular sales promotion techniques on the Web?

Some people say that the Net is nothing more than a promotion medium, similar to magazines or television. Do you agree or disagree and why?

Leveraging Technology

Rotating and Targeted Ad Banners

Hit your browser's refresh or reload button on Yahoo!'s web site and you are likely to find that the banner ad on the page changes. Yahoo! sells its inventory of banner slots on a rotating basis. Advertisers are guaranteed a certain number of impressions over a period of time but other ads will be interspersed with theirs. This is not unlike the ads that rotate on a scoreboard during professional sporting events. However, sporting events have a distinct advantage--they know the characteristics of their audience and therefore can target ads to their needs. Magazines and newspapers have a similar feature called "selective binding." Advertisers in Time Magazine, for example, can select from among over 200 different versions: any market from doctors, business executives, or students to very specific geographic areas. It is likely that the issue of Time that you receive as a student will contain different ads and even a few different articles than issues created for other markets. In order to achieve the same level of efficiency in the online world, the industry developed targeted ads. We saw these in the Search Strategies chapter. The ad changes or rotates based upon the search words that you type into the search engine. Targeted ads cost more per impression because advertisers are more effectively able to reach their target based on psychographics (interests of users).

Chapter 8
Price Planning on the Net

Marketers spend a lot of time developing pricing strategies, taking into account many variables. First is the pricing objective: profit maximization, sales maximization, status quo, or image. A profit objective usually results in high prices relative to costs. A sales objective usually results in low prices to stimulate increased consumption. Companies with status quo objectives want to price at the same levels as competition, and companies with image objectives will price either high or low depending on the desired image. For example, Rolls Royce has an image-pricing objective, pricing its automobiles at a high level to be consistent with its luxury image. The next variable is demand. A firm wants to know how many units will be sold at various price levels. Third is the cost of producing and selling a product. In order for a firm to be profitable, prices must be set at some level above costs. Exactly how much above costs is partially determined by which pricing objective drives the pricing strategy. A company's pricing strategy can be fine-tuned through tactics such as cash or volume discounts. Finally, a firm's macroenvironment must be considered: social factors, competition, the economy, and others.

Competitive Environment

Competition puts pressure on pricing levels. In a monopoly, theoretically the firm can select any price it desires. Of course, in the United States the government protects consumers by regulating pricing in monopoly companies (e.g., the utility company). The other extreme is commodity pricing. Consumers view commodity products as being fairly similar. After all, is there a real difference among brands of chlorine bleach? Commodity product pricing tends to equalize among competitors because with little product difference, price will usually be the purchase choice variable.

Commodity Pricing

New products such as Excite's shopping service (www.excite.com) make it easier for users to find the lowest prices for a particular product sold online. All you have to do is type in the CD artist, computer software, or other product name, and Excite's robot will search hundreds of electronic storefronts to give you a list of various places and prices where you can purchase it. These services have the potential to turn the Web into a price-driven market, putting additional burden on manufacturers to differentiate their products or drop prices. In the following exercise you will explore a service commodity product. Airlines are often difficult for consumers to differentiate. That is, if five airlines fly to the same destination, consumers tend to select based on price. A price driven market such as the airline industry closely resembles a commodity market.

Expedia

Learning Objectives

- Understand the role of price in commodity service markets
- Demonstrate an understanding of how pricing strategy varies with demand
- Describe the relationship of pricing to other consumer decision variables

Most consumers view airline reservations as a commodity. Consumers will often trade off other variables such as non-stop flights, preferred travel times, and choice of airline to get the lowest possible price. One notable exception is the business traveler. Business travelers often have to book at the last minute. Constrained by meeting times, they require non-stop flights and inflexible travel times. Airlines are able to charge business travelers a premium for short advance bookings, non-stop flights, and preferred travel times.

From the airline company's perspective a seat on a flight is a perishable commodity. Whether empty or loaded, it costs the same amount to fly the airplane. Therefore, airlines run complex statistical models to determine what classification and price to set each seat so as to fly as close to capacity as is possible. The science of pricing on airlines is called yield management.

In this exercise we are going to plan a round trip flight from New York City to Paris, France. We will begin by researching France.

CIA Factbook

The CIA maintains information about countries all over the world. Visit the CIA at www.odci.gov/cia. Don't be put off by their welcome message--some hackers once broke into their site and they are rather upset about it. Find their World Factbook publication on the site. Then find France.

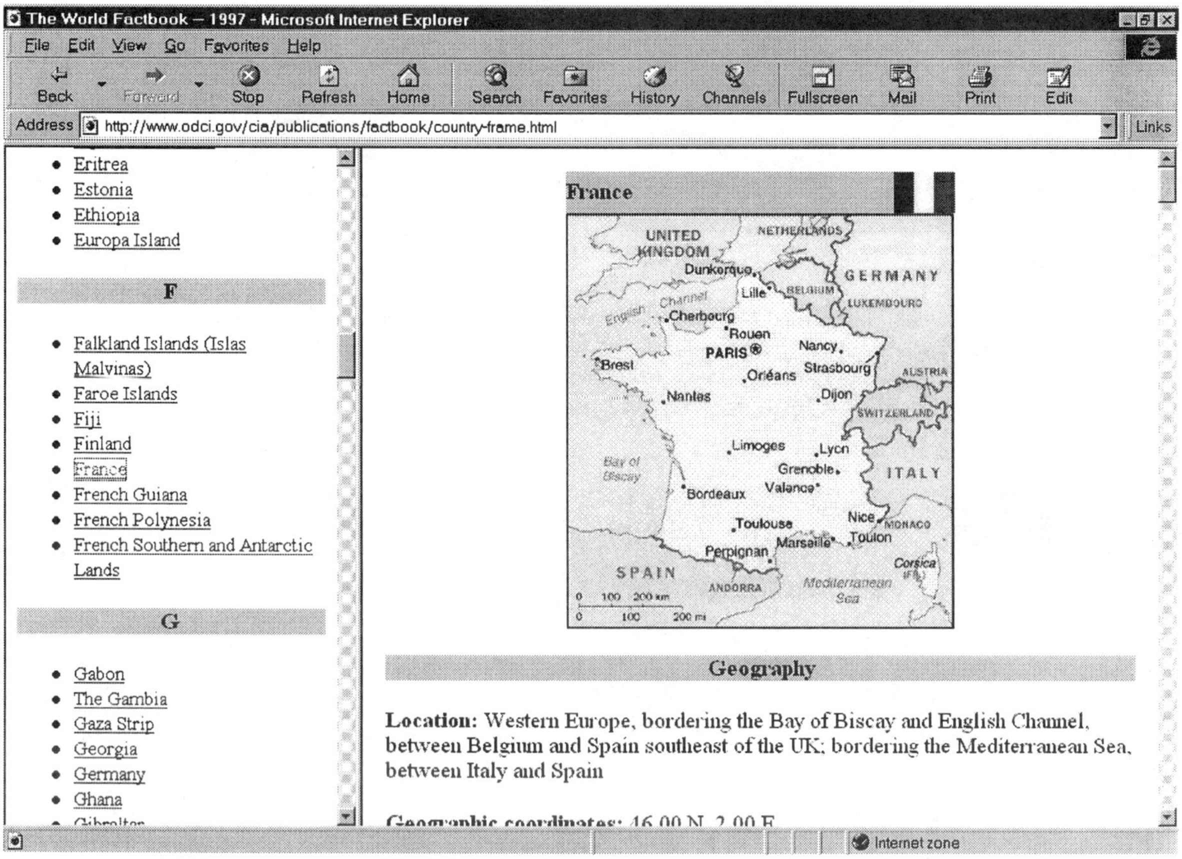

Describe the climate of France.

What is the name of its Prime Minister?

With what country does France trade most (exports and imports)?

What is the unemployment rate?

Expedia

Expedia is a product of Microsoft. The site allows consumers to book their own flights and to specify important decision criteria.

Sign onto the Expedia Web site at www.expedia.com or www.expedia.msn.com.

Follow links to Expedia Travel Agent and register a new account; it's free. Now start a new itinerary and select the flight wizard. You should end up with a screen like this:

Price a roundtrip flight from New York City to Paris traveling coach class, departing tomorrow and returning the following day. Record Expedia's response in the table below. Then press the Search Again button and vary the criteria to complete the rest of the table:

Class	Departing	Returning After	Airline & Departure Flight	Price
Coach	Tomorrow	1 day		
Coach	Tomorrow	1 week		
Coach	Next Month	1 day		
Coach	Next Month	1 week		
First	Tomorrow	1 day		
First	Tomorrow	1 week		
First	Next Month	1 day		
First	Next Month	1 week		

Based on the information you discovered, answer the following questions:

How does advance booking affect price for coach? For first class?

How does a Saturday night stay affect price for coach? For first class?

After doing this exercise, you can see why pricing in a commodity service market is very competitive. It is common for consumers to choose the lowest price when they cannot differentiate among product offerings. Services such as Expedia make it easier for consumers to do this.

Summary

Rank in order of most expensive to least expensive the three flight decision factors you explored in this exercise (advance booking, first class, Saturday stay).

How is consumer demand level taken into account in airline pricing?

What are some other commodity products that might experience similar pricing effects?

How could the airlines use the Expedia database for price planning?

Leveraging Technology

Shopping Agents

Expedia's ability to find the lowest price fare available anywhere in the world is a model being adapted to the retail industry as well. Shopping services, which can scan the Internet in search of the lowest prices, are beginning to spring up. Most of these operate in vendor alliances. For example, an agent might represent 10 different CD retailers. When the user types in the desired CD, they are presented with a list of availability of the CD among the 10 retailers and their prices! This has the obvious effect of putting a downward pressure on prices since the consumer will tend to choose the cheapest supplier, all other things being equal. There is also a psychological leveling effect of the shopping agent since the consumer can surmise that if the agent recommends the site, the site is probably reputable--otherwise why would they jeopardize their own reputation by continuing to list it? Most of the agents support one click transfer to the desired retailer. The retailers for their part may give a special discount to the consumer for having arrived via the shopping agent. This helps encourage an immediate purchase since psychologically the consumer feels that the discount may not be there on a future visit. Product inventories that are kept in digital form on the Internet create a whole new way of retailing that savvy marketers must leverage quickly or be left behind.

Appendix A

Hot Sites for Marketing Research

AltaVista	www.altavista.digital.com AltaVista is a search engine that indexes over 50 million pages on the Web.
American Demographics Marketing Tools	www.demographics.com Contains a variety of marketing publications including American Demographics Magazine.
CDT privacy	www.13x.com/cgi-bin/cdt/snoop.pl The CDT privacy demonstration page demonstrates some privacy concerns in cyberspace.
Census Bureau	www.census.gov The Census Bureau contains the greatest repository of demographic statistics concerning the United States. New facilities allow users to generate their own reports and even construct thematic maps utilizing population statistics.
CIA Factbook	www.odci.gov/cia/publications/nsolo/wfb-all.htm The CIA Factbook is one of the most authoritative sources for economic and demographic information about foreign countries.
Cyberatlas	www.cyberatlas.com Cyberatlas compiles the latest statistics on Web user characteristics and behavior from many different sources. It provides interesting articles about current trends.
DejaNews	www.dejanews.com DejaNews is one of the most inventive services on the Internet. It indexes messages posted to newsgroups and allows searches on postings.

Dell Computer	www.dell.com Dell's online storefront earns over $2 million each day! Users can configure and purchase computers online.
Excite	www.excite.com Excite is a concept based open text search engine. It accepts search strings resembling natural language. You can for example type, "demographic data on generation X."
InterNIC	www.InterNIC.net The InterNIC is where you register domain names and see which names have been registered to others.
Research-It!	www.iTools.com/research-it/research-it.html Research-It! lists a number of research sources including a dictionary, thesaurus, acronym lookup, language translation, anagram construction, biographical dictionary, Britannica's Lives, the Bible, Bartlett's quotations, maps, CIA Factbook, area codes, toll free directory, currency conversion, and stock quotes.
SRI	future.sri.com The Stanford Research Institute provides some of the best psychographic research on Web users. The site allows you to determine your own VALS and iVALS type.
Yahoo!	www.yahoo.com Yahoo! is the best-known subject tree index. The Yahoo! editors have categorized and cross-referenced tens of thousands of Web sites. In our opinion this is the best place to start when researching a topic.

Appendix B
Glossary

Banner Ad	Designated space for rent on a Web page. Banners are usually rectangular in shape and are hyperlinked to the sponsoring company's Web site.
Browser	A browser is a software program that runs on a personal computer and provides a graphical user interface (GUI) to the Web. The two most popular browsers are Netscape Navigator (or Communicator) and Microsoft Internet Explorer.
Brochureware	A Web site that contains only product and company information: an online product brochure.
Cyberspace	Cyberspace is used to describe the environment which users enter into on the Net.
Demographics	Demographics are vital statistics about people such as their age, income and ethnicity.
Domain Name	Domain names are used to address sites on the Internet. The top-level domain names are com, edu, gov, net, and org. Second level domain names usually correspond to familiar trademarks like Coca-Cola, McDonalds, Pepsi, etc.
Environmental Scan	In an environmental scan, the organization collects and interprets information about the trends, events and relationships which might affect its marketing effort.
Ethernet	Ethernet refers to the most popular transport technology standard used in local area networks (LANs).
FAQ	Frequently Asked Questions (FAQs) often appear as a link on the home pages of different sites.
Frame Relay	Frame Relay refers to the most popular transport technology standard used in wide area networks (WANs).

Home Page	A Home Page is first page that you see when you visit a site (e.g., www.honda.com). Sites often have many different home pages if they host many different users. In this case you must know the subdirectory where the users home page is located (e.g., wwwsb.ccsu.ctstateu.edu/faculty/frost/460).
Host	A host is a computer on the Web. One host can host many different Web sites. Many colleges and universities have a host available for student Web pages.
Hyperlink	Hyperlinks are text or graphics that link to other pages on the Web.
Internet	The Internet is the global inter-network of computers. Major uses of the Internet include e-mail and Web browsing.
Intranet	Intranets employ Internet technology to form home pages that are internal to a company. The Intranet serves as an easily accessible repository for corporate information--anything from strategic targets to health plans. Intranets capitalize on the fact that most organizations distribute far more information internally than they do to the outside world.
ISP	Internet Service Providers are companies that sell access to the Internet.
LAN	A Local Area Network connects computers in an organization allowing them to communicate and share resources such as printers and Internet connections.
Link	See hyperlink
Modem	A modem is a device that translates computer signals into sound waves and back again to allow two computers to communicate over a phone line. Its name comes from the fact that it modulates computer signals to sound and demodulates sound back to computer signals. Today's fastest modems receive data at about 50,000 characters per second.
Net	Net is short for Internet.

Primary Data	Primary data are information gathered for the purpose of researching a particular problem.
Random Sample	A random sample is the key to marketing research. When subjects are chosen at random then every member of the population has an equal chance of being chosen. Random samples help guarantee that the results of the sample will generalize accurately to the population.
Secondary Data	Secondary data are information that has already been collected for another purpose but helps with the current problem.
Site	A site is a home page on the Internet.
Sponsorship	A type of advertising where a company creates content and pays to place it on someone else's Web site.
Directory search	A subject tree search requires that the user navigate by progressively more specific subjects until they find the information for which they are looking.
T1	A T1 line is a high-speed telecommunications line used by larger organizations. T1 lines have 24 channels each of which can transmit 64,000 bits per second (Kbps). A fractional T1 line uses only some of the available channels.
WAN	Wide Area Networks (WANs) connect different divisions of an organization that are located across the city, across the country, or across the world from one another.
Web	The World Wide Web (WWW) defines a standard for navigating between computers on the Internet using hyperlinks.